Dedication

I dedicate this book to my son, Tyler Joshua Sigh. Tyler, I am absolutely thrilled and thankful to be chosen by God to be your mother. Son, you have taught me the true meaning of love, and it is the type of love that I am worthy of through Christ Jesus.

Baby, if I could give you the world, I would. However, I am giving you something far better and more valuable. I am giving you spiritual wealth. This gift will lead to every other type of wealth imaginable. Son, I have taught you so much about God. However, there will come a time when you will have your own personal encounter, and He will truly become your Father. Let not life, nor the opinions of the godless, freely challenge who God is to you. You do not owe anyone an explanation regarding your beliefs, so cherish and keep sacred your spiritual walk.

One day I will transition from this life back to my place of origin, and I expect to see you there at the appropriate time. Tyler, always remember that you WILL win if you faint not. Honey, God has not given you the spirit of fear, but of power and of love and of a sound mind. 2 Timothy 1:7

Lastly, I speak blessings upon your life. You are indeed the head and always above and never beneath. Your going in and coming out is forever blessed. Every generational chain has been eradicated from your life and it is solely up to you to soar. I expect nothing less than goodness to flow from your life. Failure shall NEVER be your portion because you are blood blessed.

Mommy

TABLE OF CONTENTS

Introduction 6

You Already Know 9

Woke! 14

The Plan of Redemption 21

Exposing the Enemy 33

Signs of Demonic Oppression 42

The Root of the Matter 57

Your Hand in the Matter 68

No Thank You! 75

Unbreak My Heart, Untie My Soul 87

The Holes in My Soul 94

Spiritual Sex Trafficking 99

Suffer Not a Witch to Live 114

Dreams Really Do Come True 124

The Race to the Right House 137

What About the Children? 144

You Already Know
you can't build on a demonic foundation

SANTERIA   LIMBO

SETBACKS

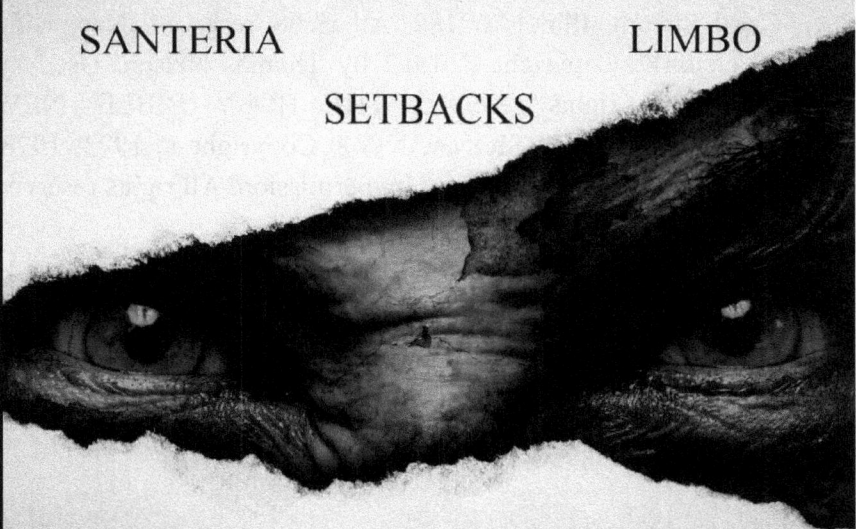

POVERTY   STAGNATION   VOODOO

DELAY   PERVERSION   ROOT

Faithe DesChamps, LICSW

This book or parts thereof may not be reproduced in any form, stored in a retrieval system, or transmitted in any form by any means — electronic, mechanical, photocopy, recording, or otherwise — without prior written permission of the publisher, except as provided by The United States of America copyright law.

Unless otherwise noted, all Scripture quotations are taken from the Holy Bible:

New Living Translation, copyright © 1996, 2004, 2015 by Tyndale House Foundation. Used by permission of Tyndale House Publishers Inc., Carol Stream, Illinois 60188. All rights reserved. New King James Version®. Copyright © 1982 by Thomas Nelson. Used by permission. All rights reserved. THE HOLY BIBLE, NEW INTERNATIONAL VERSION®, NIV® Copyright © 1973, 1978, 1984, 2011 by Biblica, Inc.® Used by permission. All rights reserved worldwide.

Copyright © 2017 Faithe DesChamps

All rights reserved.

ISBN: 978-0-692-93889-8

This Thing Called Deliverance 148

Put a Ring on Your Journey 157

Appendix A Prayers to Break Covenants 159

Appendix B Breaking Self - Imposed or Imposed Upon Curses 172

Appendix C Prayers of Renunciation 183

Appendix D Prayer Points Against Demonic Dreams 187

Introduction

I am that girl whose life was drowning in confusion, secrets, rejection, delay, blockage in multiple areas of her life. I fought through tiresome and negative cycles that didn't reflect that I was truly a child of the King. My life had gotten to a point where it seemed as though I had mastered the ability to wear masks. On the outside, it often appeared to others that I had it all together. I was told that I had the magic formula for success. After all, I came from great stock (as the old people put it). I was educated, spiritual, attractive and outgoing. I was taught that things would always work in my favor and I believed it. Ha!

My paternal-grandparents were pastors and they introduced me to ministry at a young age. As a matter of fact, my grandfather was a Bishop and, as a little girl, he often preached with me in his arms. My grandparents kept me in church and for their influence in my life, I am eternally grateful. While under their charge, I was privileged to sit at the table with many pastors and ministers alike.

I distinctly remember that the men and women of God were struggling in so many areas of their lives such as, their ministries, relationships, finances, and health. Although wonderful and truly anointed people, to me, they did not truly seem free. Besides preaching and winning souls, there was very little evidence that they were serving the true and living God. I can recall thinking, "Geesh, you guys are giving Christianity a bad reputation." I always thought that something was wrong with that picture. I believed then, and I still believe now, that Christians should win in every area of their lives.

My parents were Seventh Day Adventists and I was honored to be reared in the seventh day Sabbath truth. I embraced the SDA truth and attended two of their great schools: Oakwood University and Atlantic

Union College. However, even within the four walls of the Adventist faith, I found more of the same evidence; but in a more sophisticated manner. The Saints of God were struggling in multiple areas of their lives and covered it up with their spiritual pride, attire, and education. And as a result, the mastery of fixing or perfecting the outward versus the inward was the norm. I grew tired of covering up my pierced ears and entertaining discussions regarding why non-Sabbath keepers were hell bound when so many around me were filled with arrogance and spiritual lethargy. The spiritual pride turned my stomach! Like every sect of Christianity, there are both pros and cons. I was blessed to have been exposed to many sects of Christianity. I can say without blinking that demonic bondage can be found in the participants of them all, and so can the power of God.

In my early twenties, I remember having a dream and in it, I heard God's voice. He yelled, "Ezekiel 2." Startled, I jumped out of my sleep at the sound of His voice. I had never read Ezekiel 2 and purposed to do so immediately upon my next waking moment. I went outside and sat in my father's Chrysler, 5th Avenue. As I read the chapter, I knew that I was clearly being given instructions regarding my spiritual assignment in the earth realm. It took me twenty years to walk into it.

So much took place in those twenty years. Life happened. I pursued many dreams and goals. I experienced many personal ups and downs. I went through a very humbling process which you will gain a better understanding of as you continue reading. Even though it was a twenty year process, it was *my* process and every one of those years of development were necessary.

One of the major requests that God asked of me was to walk away from the Adventist faith. I obeyed and the critics of my journey had a field day! I didn't care because at a young age, my grandmother encouraged me to hear God for myself. I knew that God was leading me. I didn't know it then, but my obedience led to a greater appreciation of the Sabbath.

God used that time to purge me of religion, tradition and the opinions of man. As a deliverance minister, you cannot do what I do with those three monkeys on your back! Nothing escaped my hands that he didn't compensate me for. Although I doubt that I will ever commit to a traditional church setting again, during my time away, He opened my understanding to the fact that:

1. Demons are real
2. They are affecting us more than we know
3. Their legal rights and covenants to operate in our lives must be broken
4. We must enforce what Christ did on the cross by utilizing the authority He left for us in Luke 10:19
5. I can live a life of abundance while here on earth

Within the pages of this book, I will share more about my in-between journey, show you how demons directly affect us, expose the tactics and excuses that they use to do so, as well as how to use your God-given authority to break free for the sake of living the life of abundance that has been promised to us. Because of this knowledge and the implementation of the principles that I share in this book, I now win in every situation! My life is on track and I'm surrounded by peace, love and prosperity. The enemy now knows that when he comes for me, he's getting a beat down in the Spirit Realm in return. Although I'm rejoicing that things stolen from me are back in my hands, the fight is NOT over. I'm not by any means satisfied. I demand the inheritance of my mother and a seven-fold return on what was stolen. I expect all future blessings to arrive unharmed and unhindered.

Minister Faithe DesChamps. LICSW

You Already Know

Chapter 1

Hello reader. I am absolutely thrilled that you have chosen my book for your reading pleasure. This book is dangerously life changing. It will challenge and change your life for the better. I cover you now with the blood of Jesus and I pray that the Holy Spirit will guide you through this read as a teacher, revealer of truth, and deliverer.

I found it very difficult to decide where to begin while trying to determine how to structure this book. There are literally hundreds of books on spiritual warfare, and I did not desire to model my book after any of them. Actually, it was not until I opened my computer and began to type that the Holy Spirit whispered the title of my very first book: You Already Know! I instantly fell in love with the title because it encompasses my personality and ministry mandate.

I love root work and waste no time getting to the point. When I say root work, I mean getting to the core of issues. I am not a surface-level type of girl. The title goes straight to the heart of the matter, so let us be honest and not play any games with each other. You already know that something is off in your life and that is why you chose this book. In your private time and while casually talking to your inner circle, you have been scrutinizing your life, comparing your losses versus wins, examining damaging patterns, and weighing your thoughts. You have come to the startling conclusion that something is not right but you cannot confidently identify what. You love God and honor Him. You attend church faithfully and perform all that is requested of you, but for some reason you cannot shake the sinking feeling that something is, indeed, wrong.

You go to the altar week after week in hopes of reaching your breakout moment. However, your hope stops once the music does. You are a decent enough person, but it seems that your efforts do nothing to get rid of your ever-present feeling that something is holding you back. This dark cloud follows you everywhere that you go. It seems to get thicker and thicker the more you talk about it; as if it is taunting you. When you speak to your pastor, counselor, or most trusted advisor, they try their very best to give you words of comfort and motivation. Some even attempt to talk you out of what you already know. My friend, what you fail to discern is that your transparency sparked something within them that they, too, already know regarding their own life—something is not right!

Let us talk about what you already know. No matter how hard you try or how accomplished you are, you sense that there are invisible limitations, delays, and blockages that are keeping you from a life of abundance. You literally feel caged in although you are physically free. To others you may seem well put together, but little do they know that you are tormented in your mind, will, and emotions. You wrestle constantly with public and private struggles.

Although others make excuses for you by saying that everyone is struggling with something, you know that not only is your struggle real but it is strangling life from out of you. You also know that it's not normal for you to experience so much defeat, heartache, rejection, sickness, disappointment, loss, calamity, and mental torment. You are sure that something is blocking your prosperity, your womb, and both your marital and educational destinies. There has to be something dark and sinister behind your inability to enter into your settled place.

As I type this chapter, my heart is aching because I am taken back to a time when I was a hot monkey mess. I was gifted and talented, attractive, and accomplished. I was the girl that others admired. I was popular and stood out from the rest in every arena I entered. I was captain of the cheerleading squad, homecoming queen, and a member of student council. I competed in many talent contests and came out on top. I traveled the world promoting ministry. I exited my college years with two undergraduate degrees, a master's degree, and several levels of certification. In spite of all of this, I still felt as if my life was lacking something. Reflecting, I had experienced so much rejection and opposition throughout my life that I am amazed to this very day that I am still standing in sanity.

The year 2009 was the absolute worst, yet the most transformational year of my life. I faced a divorce as well as legal, character, and health issues while trying to finish graduate school, and grieve with my mother's death. I know without a doubt that I would not be here if God had not kept me. In all honesty, I contemplated suicide and had gone as far as developing a plan of execution. Thank God for grace!

Although I sensed something was seriously wrong, the year 2010 whispered relief and I tried to go about life as usual. I later found myself in a relationship with a young man that was very toxic and outside the will of God. My life was filled with many failures, struggles, and defeat. I so desperately wanted something to work in my life that I began dumbing myself down in hopes of persuading him to love me. After some very embarrassing ups and downs in our relationship, I accepted a ring from him on July 4, 2012.

Prior to this, one day as I stood in the bathroom doing my hair, I had a vision of a warrior angel of the Most High God appearing behind me. I will never forget this encounter as it was the first day of the new year, January 2012. The angel drew his sword and stated that he would be taking the next season of my life personally. He left just as suddenly as he had appeared. I immediately began to praise God, but I had no idea what the warrior angel meant by his statement. In spite of all, I accepted his message in faith. I am SO thankful to God that I did because it changed the entire trajectory of my destiny. What I do know is that, from that point forward, I had no peace whatsoever while being in that relationship. However, I still accepted the marriage proposal because it made me feel special and validated. So there I was, rocking a very beautiful and expensive ring, which was every girl's dream. I knew that I was settling but something in me would not let him go. To be honest, I was not confident that he was going to be a good husband nor was I equipped to fulfill the role of a Godly wife.

A couple of weeks later, one of my co-workers introduced me to one of Dr. Cindy Trimm's books and additional information regarding how to break free from strongholds. A dormant love for spiritual warfare was revived in me as I read, and I took the information and ran with it. I began faithfully praying the prayer Dr. Trimm outlined in her book at 3:00 a.m. every morning. More resources were given to me, and I began to feel an awakening take place in my soul.

I will never forget my greatest breakthrough, which took place on a Sunday morning. I was awakened by the Lord, and directed to take my mattress outside and pray. He revealed to me that the spirit of perversion would break free from my life as I prayed. In all honesty, I did not understand the full implication or significance of what I was being asked to do because I was still a baby in spiritual warfare. However, I followed through with a heart of obedience and a willingness to do whatever it took to put myself in a position to be a good wife and mother. What I did not know is that my decision to obey God would result in my engagement being called off and my relationship ending; never to be revived again. My world came crashing down around me, and I found myself homeless. All was not lost as a team of faithful supporters came to my rescue without question or hesitation. They packed me up and I moved in with a family from church. This transition presented the opportunity for me to be nursed back to health without interruption.

At this very moment I am laughing and screaming, "Thank you Jesus for rescuing me from myself!" During those crushing moments, I did not have much to be thankful for, but my present situation is so much better than my past. Back then, I knew that something was wrong but I was too weak, distracted, and void of resources necessary to help me face my tormented life. Hitting rock bottom forced me to self-examine, and I did not like what I saw. There was something very wrong within me and around me, and I was finally ready to confront the problem no matter the cost. I remember the day that I cried out to God, "Something is wrong!" He whispered back, "Faithe, you already know!"

Soul Work:

What is it that you already know?

Do you sense that something invisible is blocking and delaying you?

Prayer Point:

Dear God, I know that something is wrong and I am ready to discover what. Holy Spirit, speak to my heart, I am listening. Amen

Chapter Terms: Warrior Angel: *an angel of God whose specific assignment is to fight the enemies of God.*

Woke!

Chapter 3

After my engagement ended, one thing that frustrated me most was the number of people who suddenly had the boldness to tell me how much they hated my relationship. The most irritating thing is the fact that some of those same people presented a very different opinion while I was in the relationship. Inwardly, I knew that the relationship was not right and I sincerely desired someone to speak truth to me. I longed for a woman or man of God to boldly speak liberation into my broken soul, but no one did. Since then, many individuals have stated that they did not want to get involved, nor did they want to upset me. I get it!

However, taking a passive or passive-aggressive role is never appropriate if you say that you love someone. The truth is always appropriate, and assertiveness is always warranted in situations of this nature. What a person chooses to do with the truth they are presented with is a very personal matter. However, they can never say later that truth was not presented to them. Unbeknownst to my friends, I would have readily accepted their advice and listened to all that they had to share with me if only they had attempted to talk with me. I was, and still am, an exception to the rule. There is a huge difference between not getting involved and pretending that you are actually happy for someone. I have found that it is best to say and do absolutely nothing than to be dishonest.

There were instances when I expressed doubt and was reprimanded by those who I held in high regard. I now shiver at how vulnerable and impressionable I was. I was told that I was green and that I was not woman enough to handle such a man. Another sister announced in front of mutual friends that I was spoiled and ungrateful. She made this statement after I had disclosed to her the night before that I was not sure that I should follow through with getting married. I felt condemned and embarrassed by her careless and insensitive announcement.

One sister turned to me in church and prophesied that this man was indeed my husband and that I was responsible for his soul's salvation. Of course, I was excited by the first part but did not weigh the theological error of the second portion of the statement. Since when is a woman above her husband or responsible for his soul's salvation? I was even more thrown off by a "prophetic" word that was delivered by another sister in Christ, who rebuked me by stating that I was never to take the ring off again. Unbeknownst to her, I had taken off the engagement ring several times because I already knew that something was not right. As a result, I became confused by the release of that prophetic word as I truly believed that it was from God. Besides, how else could she have known? Spiritually speaking, I was definitely asleep.

Due to the knowledge that I currently possess, the answer is now obvious. Familiar spirits were behind it all. This conclusion can be confidently drawn because none of those individuals were spiritually appointed by God to speak into my life. Therefore, their words were influenced by familiar spirits designed to keep me in what God never ordained. They possessed just enough information about my personal life to give them a false sense that God had spoken to them on my behalf. Contrary to what my grandmother taught me, I dismissed the Holy Spirit's voice and embraced the false prophecies. As ridiculous as this may sound, I truly began to believe that I was ungrateful and spoiled. Reader, sometimes people will speak into your life from a place of pain and/or personal gain and call it God. Mercy! That's another book!

Now more than ever, I have a greater understanding of what my warrior angel meant when he said he would be taking the next season of my life personally. I believe God knew that I did not have a lot of truth operating in my life. I could hear Him but I deemed myself unworthy because of my brokenness, and I allowed anyone who appeared to have it together to override His voice. Asleep I was! I am very thankful that I did not stay in such a dangerous slumber. While on my journey to emotional wellness, I vowed that I would always tell myself and others the truth unapologetically. I assessed that there are too many people in this world who are willing to lie and tiptoe around the truth. I concluded that the world will gladly support subpar behavior and dysfunction because it solidifies the other person as a non-contender on the larger stage of life. To many, that person is one less rival to compete against and one less threat to the enemy. In my previous state, I was not taken seriously by many. And rightfully so, I was asleep!

Just days after my broken engagement, I was literally sick and tired of being sick and tired. I was finished making excuses for the plight of my life. I wanted out of my slumber. Reader, one evening, I sheepishly looked into the mirror and I disposed of what I saw. I saw cycles of defeat, broken relationships, rejection, depression, poverty, sexual perversion, dishonesty, delay, and limitation. I faced opposition everywhere I went. Opposition showed up in one form or another. I became distraught while examining my truth. I had lost a marriage and now an engagement. Regardless of the circumstances, I had suffered one too many unexplainable losses. I instinctually knew that I was operating under a curse and I was determined to expose and break it! The slumber was lifting! I started praying more and doing my homework. I was determined to defy the odds by walking into my wealthy place that God promised His children.

If you fully obey the Lord your God and carefully follow all his commands I give you today, the Lord your God will set you high above all the nations on earth. All these blessings will come on you and accompany you if you obey the Lord your God: You will be blessed in the city and blessed in the country. The fruit of your womb will be blessed, and the crops of your land and the young of your livestock— the calves of your herds and the lambs of your flocks. Your basket and your kneading trough will be blessed. You will be blessed when you come in and blessed when you go out. The Lord will grant that the enemies who rise up against you will be defeated before you. They will come at you from one direction but flee from you in seven. The Lord will send a blessing on your barns and on everything you put your hand to. The Lord your God will bless you in the land he is giving you. The Lord will establish you as his holy people, as he promised you on oath, if you keep the commands of the Lord your God and walk in obedience to him. Then all the peoples on earth will see that you are called by the name of the Lord, and they will fear you. The Lord will grant you abundant prosperity—in the fruit of your womb, the young of your livestock and the crops of your ground—in the land he swore to your ancestors to give you. The Lord will open the heavens, the storehouse of his bounty, to send rain on your land in season and to bless all the work of your hands. You will lend to many nations but will borrow from none. The Lord will make you the head, not the tail. If you pay attention to the commands of the Lord your God that I give you this day and carefully follow them, you will always be at the top, never at the bottom. Do not turn aside from any of the commands I give you today, to the right or to the left, following other gods and serving them. Deuteronomy 28:1-14, NIV

I was unsure of how to do it at the time, but I was determined to turn my life around. I suddenly developed a strong distaste for those operations of the church that profited my spirit nothing. I was no longer interested in church as usual. I did not want to hear another sermon, sing another song, nor produce another production. I also lost my desire to hang with the saints. I know this may seem drastic, but I felt there was more to unearth than what I had experienced spiritually. Can I be honest? I was SICK of religion! My frustration led me to divorce religion and Christianity void of demonstration. This baby was awakening but I still had a little crust in my eyes. Nevertheless, I was seeing clearer than ever! I knew that I needed power and real life-changing answers, and God did not fail to provide them.

One day while I was praying, the scripture John 10:10 came to mind. It states, *"The thief does not come except to steal, and to kill, and to destroy. I have come that they may have life and that they may have it more abundantly" (NKJV)*. The Holy Spirit began ministering to me and showed me that I was not living a life of abundance. He communicated that it is not God's will for me, or anyone else, to be enslaved to sin. He impressed upon my heart that sickness and disease do not glorify the Father. He made it clear that it is not God's will for His children to struggle to pay their bills, and to worry about food and shelter. He magnified the fact that a tormented mind is not part of God's plan of an abundant life for His children.

The Spirit also articulated that addictions of any form mock the liberating work of the cross. The Holy Spirit lovingly explained that God is no respecter of persons, as He did not send some to earth to prosper while others suffer under the iron fist of poverty and defeat. Such behavior would be contrary to God's character because He desires that His children be victorious in every area of their lives. This revelation excited me even the more and intensified my desire to dig even deeper than I had before.

The Holy Spirit began showing me that the church, as a whole, is very one-sided. It does a great job defining who Christ is and what his death, burial, and resurrection represents while ignoring the other side, the dark side. The church loves to quote John 10:10 without giving respect to the actions of the enemy. As outlined in the text, the enemy has a very powerful threefold ministry that entails stealing, killing, and destroying. The Holy Spirit also showed me that the church has adopted a very ignorant stance regarding the works of the enemy by downplaying his role by making statements such as, "Don't give the enemy too much credit." When, in fact, we do not give him enough credit.

Let's be frank, since when does knowing about your opponent by studying them translate into giving them too much credit? Here is a word of advice, you may neglect the study of your opponent but you'd better believe that your opponent is studying you. You should also know and understand that there is a file being kept on you by the enemy, and it details every aspect of your life. With this knowledge in mind, how do you seriously think you are going to defeat an enemy in which you know absolutely nothing about? You can't! The Holy Spirit also drove home the point that a lack of knowledge about spiritual warfare and an inability to operate authoritatively are the main reasons why the church is not advancing as it should on a micro, meso, and macro level. Regardless of the finished work of the cross, we have to be diligent in working the middle while embracing the fact that we have the victory.

It has been my experience that the average Christian cannot define in detail how the enemy steals, kills, and destroys when asked. Many are very disobedient to the scripture commanding the church not to be ignorant regarding the devices of the enemy. Sadly, the only devices that many of God's people are familiar with have an apple on them.

Finally, the Holy Spirit gave further revelation as to those areas of my life where the enemy was securely anchored. Reader, that joker had positioned himself comfortably to intercept the flow of blessings that rightfully belonged to me. As I sat there with my mouth agape, a righteous indignation rose within me. I was completely WOKE for the first time in my sanctified life. It was at that moment that I truly became angry and declared, *"This means war!"* The Holy Spirit whispered, *"You already know."*

Soul Work:

Are you surrounded by people who tell you the truth?

What devices has the enemy been using against you?

Prayer Point:

Heavenly Father, please expose the devices that the enemy has been using against me.

Chapter Terms: Familiar Spirit: *A spirit that knows everything about you and your family.*

The Plan of Redemption

Chapter 3

When I made the decision to be an active participant in acquiring my freedom, I literally gave myself over to the process. I purposed in my heart to learn everything I could about the enemy and his devices. I understood that no contender is ever taken seriously when the rules of engagement are unknown. One must know how to appropriately engage the enemy troubling their life. I knew that I needed the right gear, weapons, and strategy if I was going to take my life back!

One thing I learned, and rather quickly, is that the enemy is very well organized, strategic, and determined. Satan and his disciples are driven by an unimaginable force of evil. They hate you and absolutely enjoy stealing, killing, and destroying your life and that of your loved ones. It does not matter if you refuse to acknowledge them because they proudly acknowledge you. Stop playing games, you already know the truth! You cannot believe that angels are real without acknowledging demons. Unfortunately, those who insist on embracing ignorance and rebellion are losing valuable time and their inheritance of living a life of abundance.

Reader, please do not waste another moment trying to convince anyone of what you already know. As a servant of the Most High God, I am giving you permission to focus on yourself for once in your life. It is time to sober up! It is past time for you to understand the unseen war you have been enlisted in. You need to understand what you are up against and the reasons why. I encourage you to relax so that your soul and spirit are open to receive God's account of how the unseen war began and how it will end.

Who Is the War Between?

The war is between the kingdom of light in which Jehovah is king, and the kingdom of darkness in which Satan is king. Luke 10:17-18 tells the story of seventy disciples who excitedly boasted to Jesus about their ability to command demons to obey them through the authority of His name alone. They were excited because one's ability to cast out demons in that manner was absolutely unheard of prior to Jesus' arrival. The measure of authority that Jesus possessed and demonstrated was absolutely fascinating and mesmerizing to the disciples. I can see Jesus chuckling and admiring the disciples' conversation to the point that he decided to interrupt them by stating, "You think that's something? Well, I saw him fall from heaven like a bolt of lightning."

Then war broke out in heaven. Michael and his angels fought against the dragon, and the dragon and his angels fought back. But he was not strong enough, and they lost their place in heaven. The great dragon was hurled down—that ancient serpent called the devil, or Satan, who leads the whole world astray. He was hurled to the earth, and his angels with him. Revelation 12:7-9 (NIV)

What Caused the War?

The book of Ezekiel gives a really great and concluding account of what happened during that dreadful period when Lucifer decided to rebel against God. The story is mind blowing! To rebel against God, Lucifer truly bumped his head. Ha!

You were in Eden, the garden of God. Your clothing was adorned with every precious stone—red carnelian, pale-green peridot, white moonstone, blue-green beryl, onyx, green jasper, blue lapis lazuli, turquoise, and emerald—all beautifully crafted for you and set in the finest gold. They were given to you on the day you were created. I ordained and anointed you as the mighty angelic guardian. You had access to the holy mountain of God and walked among the stones of fire. You were blameless in all you did from the day you were created until the day evil was found in you. Your heart was filled with pride because of all your beauty. Your wisdom was corrupted by your love of splendor. So I threw you to the ground and exposed you to the curious gaze of kings. Ezekiel 28:13-15, 17 (NLT)

Basically, Lucifer was a beloved angel who was splendidly-created. He later became Satan, a hated fallen angel, after unrighteousness crept into his heart. He allowed his borrowed beauty, intellect, and glory to go to his head. His vanity caused him to become rebellious against God as his desire to become higher than God grew. If that was not enough, Satan convinced one-third of the heavenly angels to join him in rebelling against God. Unbeknownst to them, God would not take this lightly and they were swiftly dealt an eviction notice and cast out of heaven. The book of Isaiah gives an even more detailed account of what transpired, and it also foretells Satan's future fate. The conclusion of the matter absolutely thrills my heart and gives me LIFE!

How you have fallen from heaven, morning star, son of the dawn! You have been cast down to the earth, you who once laid low the nations! You said in your heart, "I will ascend to the heavens; I will raise my throne above the stars of God; I will sit enthroned on the mount of assembly, on the utmost heights of Mount Zaphon. I will ascend above the tops of the clouds; I will make myself like the Most High." But you are brought down to the realm of the dead, to the depths of the pit. Those who see you stare at you, they ponder your fate: "Is this the man who shook the earth and made kingdoms tremble, the man who made the world a wilderness, who overthrew its cities and would not let his captives go home?"

Isaiah 14:12-17 (NIV)

According to Revelation 12:4, Satan and those angels whom he skillfully influenced to abandon their post were cast from heaven to earth. Biblical scholars believe that when they hit earth, the impact knocked everything out of order. The earth in all of its devastation became a new home to the fallen agents of darkness. These unwanted house guests came to earth with supernatural power, but were devoid of the authority necessary to use it. For example, it is no different than a social worker being licensed in one state and then, relocating to another. The social worker has the legal authority to practice only in the state in which he/she was originally licensed. Although licensed, one's authority to practice in the new state is rendered null and void until the proper channels have been assessed and authority is granted. With that being said, Satan and the fallen angels were never licensed to practice on earth. All of their previous orders were given to them by God, who instructed them on how and when to do His business.

Satan and his crew gloried in their new found freedom as they were not accustomed to being on their own; free of structure and instruction. Since the fall, they were now in an environment where they had free-reign to do as they pleased. Leading up to the fall, Satan was closest to God out of all of the other fallen angels. He possessed intimate knowledge of God's Kingdom. With heaven as his only point of reference, Satan stole its blueprint of order and built a demonic replica that was void of God's light. His crooked works quickly introduced darkness into the earth's realm. Upon their arrival, the earth was sadly infiltrated with a darkness that was invisible, sinister, and evil. Satan brought sin, decay, disease, immorality, death, rebellion, and instability with him.

In spite of everything, one must understand that not all hope for earth and its inhabitants was lost. You must always remember that Satan and his followers possess a power that is useless without authority. With this knowledge in hand, the thief called his minions together and put into effect his newly constructed plan to steal, kill, and destroy. It was, indeed, their launching party. It pleased Satan to receive praise and adoration from Beings who were just as sick and lost as he was. This made him feel validated and kingly!

In some twisted way, he truly felt equal to God until God showed up on the scene to bring order back to the earth. I can hear his minions hackling God and saying things like, "Yeah, that's it, clean up our mess;" "Hey God, you missed a spot—you must do better than that;" "You're our slave now! Hurry up and get it done. We have work to do!" For five days, they watched God clean up their mess as they hurled insult after insult in His direction. Father God, in His infinite wisdom, said not a word nor did He act out of character. While the others were laughing, Satan was worried because he understood that God's ways are not our ways and that nothing catches Him by surprise. He knew that God was up to something and it was going to be big. Therefore, he was totally blindsided when God created man on the sixth day. The party came to a screeching halt as his evil eyes became fixated on earth's most beloved rulers, Adam and later, Eve.

Adam and Eve

The newly created beings, Adam and Eve, were not only lovingly formed by the hands of God himself, but they were also graciously created in his image and likeness. This was disheartening to Satan because every time that he looked at them, he saw the likeness of his self-made enemy, God. After bringing order and splendor to an otherwise chaotic world, the Father gave Adam and Eve dominion and authority over the earth. The Father loved and cherished them, and He made it His custom to visit them in the cool of the day. During these walks, He instructed them to be fruitful, to multiply, and to replenish the earth. In addition to this prestigious assignment, God commanded Adam and Eve not to eat the fruit found on the tree located in the middle of the garden. He also informed them that death would come upon them if they failed to comply with His request. The concept of death was completely foreign to them. They had never witnessed anything die before.

According to Genesis 3, Eve willfully made a decision to defy God's request. Being the weaker vessel of the two, she was approached by the enemy who successfully bamboozled her. Satan engaged her in conversation after he took possession of a snake's body. Many believe that the snake breed, python, was used. The serpent convinced Eve to foolishly defy the wishes of the ultimate lover and creator of her soul. Satan seduced her into rebelling against God just as he had. He skillfully coerced her into entertaining compromise by downplaying the wages of sin, which is death. He cunningly hissed through the serpent, "Eve, if you eat from this tree, you surely won't die" (Genesis 3:4). She naively fell for it and disaster struck! I truly wish that I could report that Adam did not mimic the bone of his bone and flesh of his flesh, but he did. He, too, ate of the fruit.

The glory of God that once covered their nakedness was immediately removed after they took their plunge into sin and disobedience. They instantly had their "uh oh" moment upon discovering their nakedness and experiencing emotions they had never felt before. They tried to cover themselves and hide from their friend and creator. Their disobedience instantly inducted death and decay into their beautiful world, and gave Satan the legal right to launch his multifaceted plan of destruction.

Things were completely different this time around when the Father came onto the scene. Already aware of their rebellion against Him, God reluctantly called out to His children knowing that He would be greeted with the confirmation of Adam and Eve's fallen state. I can only imagine the Father entering the Garden of Eden to find His children fearfully crouching behind a bush because they were terrified and cloaked in self-condemnation. I am flooded with emotion as I imagine His attempt to maintain His composure in front of His children who were now hiding from a God they once ran to greet. I would be devastated if Tyler, whom I carried in my tummy for nine months and nurtured through life suddenly began hiding from me. It pains me to think of losing his love and affection. How hurtful it would be to watch him lose his excitement to greet me and inquire about my plans for him and life.

The Father called out to His children, and they shamefully emerged from their hiding place wearing fig leaf garments in an attempt to hide their nakedness. Adam and Eve introduced earth's first clothing line, which was later upgraded to animal skins by their loving father. I cannot help but visualize the devilish grin plastered on the serpent's face as Satan manipulated his body, and proclaimed to the God of this universe, "Got'cha!" We all know that the easiest and quickest way to get to a parent is through their child. That low down, lying dog, Satan laughed hysterically because he knew Adam and Eve had illegally shared their dominion and authority with him upon disobeying God. I can see him boldly chanting in God's face, "Whose house? Our house!" Within the snap of a finger, God became an unwelcomed visitor in a world that He and He alone created.

Not So Fast

Just as in every great movie, evil never has the upper hand no matter the amount of losses or how desperately bad things appear. Even as Adam and Eve were informed that they had to leave their beloved home, a very disappointed yet redemptive God held His head high because His heart was drawn to His most prized possession–His son Jesus Christ. Although Satan felt victorious this round, he was ignorant to the fact that nothing catches God by surprise. Absolutely nothing!

Written into the universal script of life was a plan of redemption. So when the children of God fell, Jesus stood up in the presence of the heavenly host and proclaimed, "Not so fast! Father, let not your heart be troubled! I know very well what sin demands, and that is death. I am willing to die for them. Send me, I'll go! I'll die in order to redeem them from the hands of our enemy." As Satan and his crew taunted God, they were interrupted by a very stern and piercing look from their creator that instantly shut them up. The moment the heavenly host had been waiting on had arrived. The Most High God was ready to give His inaugural speech as redeemer and savior by stating, *"I will put enmity between you and the woman, and between your seed and her Seed; He shall bruise your head, and you shall bruise His heel"* (Genesis 3:15, NKJV).

Satan became furious because he was convinced that he had outsmarted God. Due to the fact that darkness cannot comprehend or receive revelation, Satan was oblivious to the full scope of the prophecy. However, he knew that the outcome would not be favorable because the almighty Father initiated a plan to redeem His babies and He would not fail. Satan hung his head because he knew that he was no match for God. His hate for God intensified even the more as a result of this. He called another meeting with his principalities, powers, and rulers where he pronounced a curse of damnation over all of humanity. His vicious antics magnified the evil in his kingdom to such an extent that it has yet to be quieted. His mission is no secret as his sole intent is to destroy anything that carries the glory of God. Beloved, it is no secret that Satan wants to destroy you and I!

Fulfillment of the Prophecy

Thousands of years later, as prophesied in Isaiah 7:14, a virgin named Mary supernaturally conceived a child orchestrated by the Holy Spirit. That baby turned out to be the long-awaited Messiah, Jesus Christ.

Upon His arrival, Jesus found his people in bondage to sin, religiosity, and the Romans. He walked into a class system that favored the wealthy and disqualified all others. The stench of poverty and disease tainted the air. The once beautiful and vibrant colors of nature were dull in comparison to heaven. He found human beings loving and worshipping themselves and each other. Sexual immorality was rampant, and the land was filled with false gods that were exalted above the one and only living God.

The men and women of earth may not have recognized divinity wrapped in flesh, but their mortal enemy did. Satan knew exactly who Jesus was and tried to snuff out his life as soon it began (see Matthew 2). Thank God that none of his weapons worked. God the Father pronounced at Jesus' baptism that he was indeed the Lamb of God and He sealed his approval with the Holy Spirit resting on him in the form of a dove.

Satan became desperate but not desperate enough to act prematurely. He patiently waited and finally approached Jesus at a time when he considered him to be at his weakest, at the conclusion of his 40-day fast. He tried to tempt Jesus with riches, possessions, and status but Jesus utilized one of the weapon of his warfare, scripture, to silence him (see Matthew 3 & 4). Satan later used Peter, one of the disciples, to rebuke Jesus after he witnessed the Savior healing the sick, feeding the hungry, and restoring the brokenhearted. This plan backfired and resulted in Satan getting rebuked (see Mark 8). When all else failed, he hired Jesus' treasurer, Judas, to betray his master for thirty pieces of silver. Judas' betrayal led Jesus down a trail of humiliation that ultimately led to the public crucifixion of the Savior (see Mathew 26 & 27). This was Satan's most treasured victory yet.

While Satan's minions rejoiced, he himself remained silent and focused because he knew that the power of redemption was not in

Jesus' death alone, but also in the promise of his resurrection.. I personally believe that Satan himself stood at the entrance of Jesus' grave in order to ensure that he did not get up. I can also see the tombstone laughing and mocking Satan as it taunted, "Let the countdown begin! You're nothing more than a fallen angel, and certainly no match for the King of Kings and Lord of Lords." I believe the tomb's mockery of Satan caused all of his pride, rejection, and insecurity issues to flood to the surface in a raging wave of mixed emotions. At the moment when he was on the brink of a full psychotic break down, death shook him and informed him that he need to immediately report to the lower regions of the earth.

Taking Back What the Enemy Stole

In my sanctified imagination, I can clearly see Satan arriving on the scene just in time to witness Christ using his authority and dominion to overthrow the kingdom of darkness at the appointed time. The plan of redemption was in full effect. Glowing in majesty and power, Christ snatched back the keys to death, hell, and the grave. It was such a beautiful sight because there was absolutely nothing that Satan or his minions could do about it.

Adam and Eve had an outstanding debt that was transferred to all of their descendants (including us) when they sinned, and death was the required payment. A death curse rested on the bloodline of humanity until payment was rendered in full. The death curse was permanently broken upon Christ's fulfillment of his promise to die on our behalf. Big brother Jesus paid the ultimate price for the wages of sin, thus rendering the death contract null and void (see Hebrews 2:14). Jesus' death and resurrection also reclaimed man's shared and lost sense of authority and dominion from the enemy's hands.

Upon Jesus rising from the grave and showing himself to the disciples, Jesus happily informed them that, *"All authority in heaven and on earth has been given to me. Therefore go and make disciples of all nations, baptizing them in the name of the Father and of the Son and of the Holy Spirit"* (Matthew 28:18, 19, NIV). Therefore, Satan can no longer hold a person hostage to the wages of sin even though he still claims the earth as his. Accepting Christ as one's Lord and Savior completely strips Satan of any legal rights he had as a hostage taker. Once a person gives their life to Christ, they denounce Satan's claim of ownership and boldly declare that they belong to God. By taking back control and submitting to God, they are exercising their authority and dominion over Satan and his minions. This is the same power that Adam and Eve originally possessed while in the Garden of Eden. Believers have ALL power over the enemy, and the added bonus is that nothing shall by any means harm them.

Christ remained with the disciples a little while longer. Upon transitioning back to heaven, he instructed them to remain in the upper room until the Holy Spirit came. He went back home and presented his finished works to God the Father. In my sanctified mind, just before his ascension, Jesus heard a familiar voice calling His name and asking, "Jesus, I truly messed up didn't I?" Christ responded matter-of-factly, *"Satan, you already know!"*

Soul Work: *Do you have any secrets that you are trying to hide from God?*

Why aren't you using your dominion and authority if Christ has snatched it back from the enemy?

Prayer Point:

God, I want to learn how to utilize the authority and power that I inherited from you. Amen

Chapter Terms:

Demons: Demons are believed to be the disembodied spirits of the children of fallen angels and humans that were destroyed during the flood. Their physical bodies were destroyed but not their spirit. They take orders from fallen angels and witches. As a result of being disembodied spirits, they roam around looking for a human body to live in. Their main purpose is to steal, kill, and destroy in the lives of humans.

Exposing the Enemy

Chapter 4

I am sure that you are now pondering, "Why should we be cognizant of Satan, or even care about what he is doing if Jesus' death, burial, and resurrection snatched us from the enemy's grip? Doesn't the Bible clearly state that the enemy is under our feet and that no weapons formed against us shall prosper?" I can hear you clearly stating, "No offense Minister Faithe, but it sounds to me that you are glorifying the devil over God."

Ha! There is no offense taken. You are thinking my friend, and I absolutely love it! In an effort to encourage further evaluation of this situation, I would like to pose some questions to you. Do you often wonder why you are meeting defeat in so many areas of your life? Do you often find yourself saying, "If it's not one thing, it's another!" Do you regularly question God by asking, "Why are the enemy's weapons formed against me prospering?" After all, you love God and you are doing everything within your power to honor Him but you just cannot seem to break free from whatever it is that is oppressing you. I want you to drop your religious microphone for just a moment, go to a quiet space, and let's examine your life.

I am aware that we will face problems while in this world, but do you truly believe that your losing streak is God's chosen path for your life? Do you honestly believe that being bound by sexual perversion, drugs, alcohol, perpetual rejection, poverty, legal issues, barrenness, psychological and emotional torment, and horrific nightmares is God's portion for your life? Do you believe that the condition of your family pleases God? If so, I want you to provide an explanation of how God is being glorified by your oppression. Let me spare you some time, you cannot. What I described are simply some of the devices of the enemy.

Devices are the methods that the enemy uses to attack you and keep you bound so that you can NEVER realize your full potential while on earth.

Jesus Is For You

Before we go any further, we must address that beautiful man named Jesus. Do you realize that he loves you, is for you, and not against you? You must understand that your oppression is not his handiwork or punishment for you being less than perfect. As a matter of fact, your oppression contradicts what Jesus echoed from the prophetic book of Isaiah:

The Spirit of the Lord is on me, because he has anointed me to proclaim good news to the poor. He has sent me to proclaim freedom for the prisoners and recovery of sight for the blind, to set the oppressed free, to proclaim the year of the Lord's favor. Luke 4:19 (NIV)

Why would Jesus send anything to oppress you when He is all about you living a life of freedom? If I do not impress upon you anything else of value, I want you to know and understand that Jesus is NOT mad at you. As a matter of fact, he wrote you a beautiful love letter in Jeremiah 29:11 and it reads, *"For I know the thoughts that I think toward you, says the Lord, thoughts of peace and not of evil, to give you a future and a hope"* (NKJV).

Jesus, the all-knowing son of God, considered your entire life story and still decided to die for you. Nothing you can say or do will ever take him by surprise. In his heart, you were and still are worth every thorn that was pounded into his skull, and every nail that pierced his hands and feet. He carried the weight of sin and endured being briefly forsaken by his Father just for you. He knows you by name and has numbered every strand of hair on your head. He desires to see you win, and this is why he willingly sacrificed his life for you.

I know for many of you, the saints of old told you that, "God will make all things work together for your good" (Romans 8:28). However, it does not mean that "thing" came from Him even though He has a way of making things work for your good. For example, growing up in poverty may have taught you a thing or two about humility and doing more with less, but poverty is certainly not God's will for your life.

Is He A Liar?

By now you know I like to ask questions, so here we go again!

1. Was Jesus lying when He stated through the servant that He wishes above all things that you would prosper and be in good health as your soul prospers? (See 3 John 2)
2. Was He lying when He stated that by his stripes we are healed? (See 1 Peter 2:24)
3. Was He lying when He said he would lift up a standard when the enemy comes in like a flood? (See Isaiah 59:19)
4. Was He lying when He said that you are the head and not the tail, the lender and not the borrower, above and not beneath? (See Deuteronomy 28:12, 13)
5. Was He lying when He said that if you speak to a mountain and command it to be cast into the sea, it will obey? (See Mark 11:23)
6. Was He lying when He told you that you have been given power over the enemy? (See Luke 10:19)

Now that we have completed our research, I think the appropriate answer to the question at hand is… I THINK NOT!

Keeping It Real

In your present state, you are currently an ill-equipped contender for the enemy. Why? It is very simple! You do not know the devices of the enemy because you are ignorant of them. I am also quite confident that you do not know your spiritual rights, and you certainly have not been enforcing them even if you do. In your mind you believe that you cannot win while on earth but heaven will be your just reward for enduring this cold, cruel world. No one has ever taught you that you are a spirit being, your earthly body is but a shell, and earth is not your place of origin. You existed in God long before being released to the earth. Not only are you from a heavenly kingdom, but you are here on assignment.

Do you realize that you are God's mouthpiece in the earth's realm? He accomplishes His desires through those who accept Him and partner with Him. I think it would be rather challenging to hear God and complete your Godly assignment while being oppressed by demons and overwhelming obstacles. My friends, having the belief that God can transform your life by using darkness alone is the same as believing that He is darkness. It would be the same as believing that He is part God and devil. Nonsense! The adversary is committed to taking you down, but God is committed to taking you up. Your awareness of these essential truths in addition to your actions will determine how high or low you go in life.

Scriptures on the spirit:

- I Thessalonians 5:23 • Matthew 10:28 • Ecclesiastes 12:7 • James 2:26 • Hebrews 4:12 • Galatians 5:16-17 • Genesis 2:7 • I Corinthians 6:19-20 • Romans 12:1-21 • Matthew 16:26 • I Thessalonians 4:13-17 • Luke 1:46-47 • John 3:6 • 2 Corinthians 5:6-8 • John 14: 1-3

The Rules of Engagement

My friend, I used to think just like you do until I was educated on the rules of spiritual engagement. Knowledge is the difference between merely living and living life more abundantly. Please do not rush through this section. Take your time and let the words sink beyond your head and into your heart. The work of the cross is indeed finished and we play a major role in upholding and enforcing that finished work. As discussed earlier in this book, both kingdoms are very organized and operate according to a certain set of rules. As the rules of engagement dictate, each kingdom respects the rules established within the other's kingdom. Wait one minute before you throw down this book, and please hear me out!

Satan is a legalist. He passionately studies every intricate detail of your life. He takes note of every single mistake you make and presents it to God as justification for slandering your name and oppressing you. The word of God tells us that he accuses us before God night and day (see Revelation 12:10). He knows the Bible, and he eagerly strikes when your life is not aligned with the word of God. He uses your actions against you to support his argument that you have given him a legal right to oppress you and/or your bloodline.

Satan is indeed the preferred god of this world, and those who do not accept Christ as their personal savior are his children (see John 8:44-45). Whether they realize it or not, he is claiming them on his taxes. However, people disown Satan when they decide to give their lives to Christ and join the family of God. That one decision alone gives God the right to claim them on His taxes. It also ushers them into a higher tax bracket with the return being eternal life. Beloved, I hate to inform you of this but changing tax brackets does not make you exempt from fighting in this unseen war. In all reality, the heat is now turned up even more because the enemy's attention is drawn to you like never before. You are a traitor in his eyes, and he is not going to leave you alone or get out of your body just because you are now a Christian!

You Can't Hide

Are you aware that accepting Christ as your Lord secures your seat in heaven, but does not miraculously free you from certain levels of demonic oppression? Many of these oppressions were placed upon you by your ancestors, whom you have never met, or by demons you invited in by making poor decisions throughout your life. In order to break free from the root up, demonic covenants made by you, on your behalf, and on the behalf of your bloodline must be identified and verbally broken.

For example, you may currently be renting but decide to purchase a home. Your decision to purchase a new home does not free you from your renter's agreement because you are still under a legal and binding contract with your landlord. You are free to pack and leave without giving your landlord notice, but there will be consequences following your actions because you are under contract. Those who escape without stress are those who go through the appropriate channels of breaking the contract, and so it stands in the spiritual realm. Contrary to what you have been taught, becoming a Christian does not automatically break demonic covenants, and that is why you can be devoted to Christ and oppressed at the same time.

If the enemy cannot deter you from choosing God over himself, then he will do his very best to ensure that you will not live your life more abundantly while on this earth. Let's be clear, Satan is nothing like God. Contrary to God, he does not mind sharing your worship as long as you remain nothing more than a religious zombie. He ultimately desires that you spend eternity in hell with him but once he realizes that he cannot make hell reservations for you, he does whatever he can to frustrate your destiny. He definitely does not mind you going to church, performing your rituals, misquoting and failing to enforce scriptures while embracing your clichés because none of this is effective in destroying his kingdom. He will forever remain content as long as you do not use your weapons of spiritual warfare appropriately and walk in your God-ordained spiritual authority. Satan will cheer you on as you shout, speak in tongues, and do back flips at the altar. He is awesome and very dependable support because, just like God, he wants your affection. Therefore, he's constantly in your face. He's your personal evil cheering section because he knows that he can snatch your blessings away just as soon as they are released when there is a legal right in place.

Demonic Oppression Is Real

You can keep thinking it is a game if you want, but our forefathers in the Garden of Eden were warned to stay away from the tree, but they did not. We, too, have also been warned against being ignorant concerning the devices of the enemy. Jesus drove his point home when he said, "The enemy is like a roaring lion going around looking for whomever he can devour" (see 1 Peter 5:8). My friend, who or what is he looking for? Let me help you out—he is looking for the defenseless and ignorant; especially defenseless and ignorant Christians.

He does not care what church you are a member of, nor does he care about your accomplishments. He hates you and loves to oppress you. He makes a mockery out of your life just to get back at God. He loves it when your nature reflects his more than the nature of Christ. That con artist wants your worship, and he wants to block God's glory in your life. He likes to see you cry. Watching you struggle and blame God for his works is his absolute delight. He accuses you before the Father, and you in turn, accuse the Father of not loving or defending you. How heartbreaking this must be to Father God, especially when

He has empowered you with the ability to trample on the works of the enemy as written in Luke 10:19! My friend, whoever is stealing, killing, and destroying in your life is indeed your enemy. I can hear you asking, "Can it really be true that the enemy is behind my torment?" Let me help you out, lift your hands and tell the Lord thank you because, you already know!

Soul Work:

How is God glorified by bondage?

Reflect, do you truly believe that God loves you?

Prayer Point:

I command every force that has me bound to be exposed and devoured in the name of Jesus.

Chapter Terms:

Demonic Covenants*: agreements that are made with forces of darkness knowingly or unknowingly as a result of knowingly or unknowingly tampering with what belongs to the enemy.* ***Spiritual Warfare:*** *understanding the operations of how the kingdom of darkness and light operate, and thusly, using the strategies of light to eradicate the influence of darkness operating in your life.* ***Weapons of Spiritual Warfare:*** *spiritual acts that Christians do to actively fight the enemy.* ***Legal Right****: a sin that has been committed by the person or their ancestors that the enemy uses as justification for attacking a person's life.* ***Spiritual Authority****: spiritual rights which are the specific instructions that God left regarding who we are in Him, what power we possess, and how to effectively deal with the powers of darkness.*

Heavenly Kingdom: *Heaven is the name of God's kingdom and it is where every single human being originates from.*

Signs of Demonic Oppression

Chapter 5

I know that examining your life is not fun especially when you do not like what you see, and you feel powerless to change it. How do you find comfort when it seems as if you are always struggling while others appear to be on easy street? Day in and day out, you put on your happy face and try your best to dress the part even though you know that it is all a facade. Tell the truth, you are sick and tired of hearing what Christianity has to offer when your life is so crappy. You have been told repeatedly to stop complaining because it could be so much worse, but not even that cliché brings comfort to your aching soul or dwindling destiny. Let me remind you that I can identify with your struggles because I was once in the same position. The only thing that satisfied me was the truth, and I was not set free until I took ownership of my truth.

As a matter of fact, when I first started studying spiritual warfare, a "Christian" woman told me to back off because demons do not play. I remember looking at her with utter disgust while thinking, "Aren't you a child of the Most High God?" Her cowardice angered me. Who would not want to drive out what should not be living inside their temple? Her comment fueled my hunger to learn all the more. I was not the same Faithe. I was WOKE and growing more confident in my ability to hear God for myself. I knew God was leading me, and that was the only approval that I needed. The opinions and warnings of scary, Bible-toting Christians was not enough to make me back down.

Many called me crazy because my passion for spiritual warfare made them uncomfortable and suspicious of me. This only lasted for a season, and for a while there was absolutely no one to talk to about the beautiful truths that I was discovering. I cannot tell you the number of people that I drove away before I understood that not everyone could handle the topic of demonology. At the right time, God sent a wonderful man of God to befriend me so that I could accept my calling and become comfortable in my own skin. Life began to make more sense, and I began to flourish in my God-ordained place of freedom under his mentorship.

Playing on the title of this book, let us talk specifically about what you already know. You have arrived at the startling conclusion that you are under demonic oppression. As you examine your life, you are more than likely becoming frustrated because you do not have anyone to talk to about your discovery. You know that you are ready to break free, but you are completely unsure of how to do it. You cannot go to your pastor because this information is not being taught in your church. And if it is, it is on a surface level. I can truly relate to where you are, and I have great news for you!

You, my friend, are just like the prodigal addict on the road to recovery. The very first step is recognizing and admitting that you have a problem. You are exactly where I was when God confirmed my suspicions and catapulted me into this truth. You can rest in knowing that God will never expose a problem that He is not ready to handle. My journey officially began in August 2012, and I am writing these words in November 2016. I am now in ministry full time. I help men and women of God worldwide break free from demonic oppression and heal from soul issues. I absolutely LOVE what I do! I cannot imagine doing anything different.

Please allow me to share with you nineteen areas that may indicate that you or someone you know is under demonic oppression and in need of deliverance. When working with clients, these are some of the areas I examine during my assessment in order to diagnose what demons are at work as well as how they got there. Please keep in mind that there are always exception. The following list will be valuable only to those who are active participants in their deliverance, and are doing their absolute best to live a life of abundance but keep meeting resistance. The list below is not designed to convince anyone that spiritual warfare is real but to bear witness to those of you who already know!

1. Poverty

The inability to get ahead financially is an issue many people face. However, there is a level of financial struggle that is beyond the realm of comprehension. It keeps the person in a perpetual cycle of financial highs and lows. To spiritually untrained eyes and ears, these individuals appear to be irresponsible or lacking in ambition; especially when consideration is not being given to the curse of poverty that is operating in their lives. Interestingly enough, a person can have money and still suffer from the curse of poverty. Poverty destroys more than your finances. This spirit literally sucks the life out of your creativity, opportunities of advance and ability to generate lasting wealth. Chronic signs that you are operating under a poverty curse may include:

- The inability to find employment no matter how qualified you are.
- Honorably working the same job for a respectable amount of time without any prospects of being promoted or considered for promotion.
- An unexplainable and excessive drive to spend money.
- Racking up new debt in order to satisfy current debt.
- Filing for bankruptcy.
- The accumulation of excessive overdraft and late fees due to misunderstandings or unexpected expenses.
- Borrowing from loan shark companies.

- Always paying astronomical interest rates.
- The inability to save money, and when you do, something happens to devour it.
- Living from paycheck to paycheck with no hope of it changing.
- The inability to settle down; always moving from residence to residence.
- The unseen but perceived "NO" when it comes to owning versus renting.
- Dreams of finding coins, spending money, ants, and/or losing money.
- Family losing their wealth at an age when it is impossible to retrieve.
- Comfortable living in a filthy or unclean environment.
- The ability to trace poverty patterns throughout the bloodline.

2. Cycles of Defeat

Individuals experiencing this type of demonic oppression experience cycles of defeat in noticeable areas of their life. Regardless of how hard they try, like clockwork, things go well for a while and then fall apart for bazaar and non-logical reasons. When blessings come, they become paranoid and can be found looking over their shoulders because they know their victory will be short-lived. It is hard for anyone to relax and enjoy the fruit of their labor when under such a curse. Others can be heard whispering in the midst of their success, "I wonder how long this is going to last?"

3. Limitations

These individuals are filled with dreams and visions, but sense that there is an unseen wall surrounding them that blocks their progress and success. The moment they pick up momentum, they run into unseen barriers, and experience feelings of being encaged and suffocated by unseen forces. Although going backwards is not an option, it is extremely difficult for them to freely move forward and upward. While others seem to advance in life easily, they fight tooth and nail for every inch of advancement. They sense that there are limitations on how far they can go in specific areas of life. For example, they can remain an employer but never achieve the status of supervisor. They can make 20,000 a year and no more. They can rent and never buy. The demonic barriers prevent them from advancing past a predetermined level. And when they try, they meet unprecedented warfare.

4. Chronic Delay

Indications of delay are evident in a person's life when they and others sense that certain life events should have occurred by now. A life plagued by delay allows a person to get close to achieving their goals and then denies them access by delaying them. Things that should happen easily are met with mysterious opposition causing the goal to be postponed, frustrated or aborted. Delay adds more time to what should belong to a person now or at a measurable set time. Delay specializes in sending hindrances and setbacks to frustrate a person right at the brink of breakthrough. This is done in hopes that the individual will abandon their goal or expectation. Delay desires that they will be in no position emotionally to enjoy the fruit of their hopes and desires by the time of arrival. For example, a 30-day project will somehow take three months or three years to complete. Just like the spirit of rejection, delay is a whoredom spirit that all demonic entities use. Please note that delay can be sent by God. However, one will know that God is not a part of the delay by the restlessness of their spirit man versus their flesh.

5. Demonic Hauntings

Many people who experience demonic hauntings initially feel as though they are crazy and imagining things. And to make matters worse, they usually do not have anyone to talk to about what is happening to them behind closed doors. These people report occurrences such as:

- Hearing mysterious footsteps or voices in the home.
- The doorbell ringing and/or knocking at the door only to find no one is there.
- Objects falling or mysteriously disappearing.
- Hearing their name called only to discover that no one is there.
- A strange smell of fire, sulfur or cigarette smoke with no trace of its origin.
- A bizarre sense that someone is watching them sometimes followed by goosebumps.
- Seeing spirits or shadows walking throughout the home or following them.
- Feeling someone touching them but no one is there.
- Levitating, sleep walking, and/or holding an in-depth conversation with an unseen person while asleep.
- Varying temperatures. One area or room in the home may be unexplainably cold or hot.

6. Demonic Dreams

I have devoted an entire chapter to dreams but will briefly touch on the topic here. Dreams can often indicate demonic oppression. Here are a few signs of demonic oppression that are revealed in one's dreams:

- Being chased, fought, or shot at.
- Being attacked or followed by animals.
- Experiences of being held down by an unseen force while sleeping.
- Having horrific nightmares.
- Seeing demons and dead relatives.

- Seeing yourself being driven around by an unknown person.
- Being fed by unknown people.
- Traveling to unknown destinations and being surrounded by unknown people.
- Waking up in pain and/or with bruises or marks on your body.
- Dreams of death or seeing coffins.

7. Chronic Accidents

Believe it or not, there are people who are prone to accidents of all manner. They get over one accident and are involved in another a few months later. The cycle seems to be never ending. As the story always goes, they barely escaped or should have died but somehow did not. Fender benders and scratches are the norm for them. These same people often experience perplexing product damages. When they get a new phone, they inevitably drop it and crack the screen. New computers or gadgets are subject to unexpected crashes or something similar. They start important projects which disappear at the most inopportune times. House fires, flooding, and broken bones seem to be a normal part of life, These people are often heard muttering, "I feel like I'm cursed."

8. Addictions

These individuals are driven by desires they cannot control. No matter how strong their willpower, the drive to do wrong overpowers their will to do right with such force that they succumb under the pressure. While focused on something else, unseen forces demand that they stop and obey the urge to feed the addiction. The desire to feed the addiction is so strong that these individuals show no regard for their disappointed loved ones or abandoned commitments. Obedience to the addiction typically leaves them feeling powerless, guilt-laden, and ashamed. There are times they are able to go for a season without giving in, but the urge comes back stronger than ever and they relapse. Addictions can be present in the following categories and many more: sex, drugs, alcohol, food, shopping, television, internet, and gambling. Regardless of the various scientific and medical explanations for addictions, you already know! Nothing has a right to control you.

9. Demonic Emotional Turmoil

Individuals experiencing demonic-emotional turmoil can never seem to get a grasp on their emotional well-being. It seems as though they are always on a chronic emotional rollercoaster, up one minute and down the next. Emotional instability is a normal part of their everyday life. Signs of emotional turmoil include:

- Inner conflict that manifests through cycles of despondency, hopelessness, depression, anxiety, and fear.
- Inner promotion of self-rejection and the fear of being rejected.
- Harassing thoughts that make a person suspicious of others. Eventually, they are driven into emotional and physical seclusion.
- Suggestive inner thoughts and voices that mock failure and defeat; encourage self-harm, chronic thoughts of suicide, and in some cases, murder.
- Unjustly taking offense.
- Uncontrollable jealousy and envy.
- Feelings of loneliness even when surrounded by people who love them.

10. Unexplainable Chronic Health Issues

No matter how hard they try to eat healthy and/or exercise, these individuals experience sickness and disease at an extremely alarming rate. It seems as if they are always sick and spend just as much time in the doctor's office as they do anywhere else. Some may even acquire a seemingly overnight sickness after a horrific dream of being bitten or injected by an entity. Health issues experienced by these individuals may include:

- Unexplainable pains running throughout their body; often in the back and neck.
- Sickness that seems to appear overnight and has absolutely no medical explanation.
- Swelling of the stomach, boils all over the body, and loss of hair.
- A pattern of the same sicknesses and diseases in the family.
- Feeling worn out and tired no matter how much rest one gets.
- Chronic itching is one that is often overlooked.

11. Chronic Rejection

People suffering from chronic rejection issues report that people are unjustifiably suspicious, distrustful, or jealous of them everywhere that they go. When asked why, they nor the others involved can explain why. They are often excluded from being invited to social gatherings or to participate on planning committees highlighting their expertise. Others are preferred and chosen over them regardless of their qualifications. Their kindness is often dismissed or misinterpreted. Their pure motives are often questioned, and their shortcomings are magnified. They seem to gravitate towards people who will eventually betray them or disconnect from them for trivial reasons. Even when they excel, they are not rewarded or applauded. Their accomplishments are often overlooked or watered down by others. These individuals often feel forgotten and invisible to the world.

I've devoted an entire chapter to the spirit of rejection entitled, No Thank You.

12. Chronic Family Dysfunction

When you examine your family, you find total chaos. Family gatherings end in fights or arguments. They are inundated with foul language, ratchet music, drugs, and alcohol. God is not the center of the family, and there is no unity. The family is filled with cliques exhibiting the haves and have nots. There are family members who openly practice witchcraft or downplay God's sovereignty. Domestic violence and poor boundaries are acceptable. Rumors of illegitimate children, adultery and child abuse circulate unchallenged within the family. Sexual perversion, including incest plagues the bloodline. Criminal activity, poverty, sickness, and obesity are accepted as part of the family brand. The bloodline has few or no sound marriages, and children born out of wedlock is the norm. If you are the generational curse breaker, you may feel like the black sheep of the family and that you do not belong no matter how hard you try to fit in.

13. Chronic Romantic Relational Issues

These people cannot get a romantic relationship to prosper, and have experienced heartbreak after heartbreak. They can easily get involved in purely sexual relationships, but no one will commit to them long term. A few came close to marriage, but experienced betrayal or a broken engagement instead. If they were able to get married, it was filled with unexplainable turmoil and ended in divorce. Things go great for a season but turned ugly all too quickly. It's a familiar and ugly cycle. When they examine their bloodline they see that there is a pattern of divorce and very few members of the family get and stay married. The women in the family have multiple children but have been denied the beautiful gift of marriage. The men are promiscuous and rarely settle down with just one woman.

These same individuals may have frequent dreams of former lovers, dreams of having sex with a known or unknown person, or dreams of marrying an unknown person. They may dream about nursing a baby or taking care of children that they perceive are theirs. They may experience an unknown force descending upon them and having sex with them at night while they are asleep, or during the day while they are awake. They may often awake aroused or find that they had an orgasm during a sexual dream. Others may awake feeling violated sexually or in pain, as if they were engaged in very rough sex. Other signs may include an unquenchable drive for sex and an embarrassing proclivity towards sexual perversion.

I've devoted a chapter to further exploring this topic entitled, Spiritual Sex Trafficking.

14. Chronic Sexual Humiliation

This is a pattern that I noticed among many of the women whom I had the pleasure of counseling. These women were often molested as young girls by a stranger, family member and/or a family friend. They experienced sexual disrespect from the neighborhood, church and school boys. As they grew older, some became victims of rape, on more than one occasion, at the hands of men they trusted or did not know.

Unfortunately, many of the sexual violations continued even within their committed relationships; including marriage. They suffered even further humiliation as their bedroom secrets are shared by their lovers with no personal regard to their feelings. They are forced to engage in humiliating and dehumanizing sexual acts. It is as if they have been marked to be violated and embarrassed sexually. These individuals unknowingly are marked to attract disrespect, dishonor and shame. Sadly, the concept of love making is a foreign concept because sexual disrespect has always been their portion.

15. Chronic Womb & Fertility Issues

Fertility issues, amongst males and females, is one area where people fail to consider as demonic oppression. These signs show up through unexplainable miscarriages, barrenness, painful pregnancies, low sperm count, impotency, premature ejaculation, fibroids, and painful menses. A female may experience mysterious pain during sex, especially during sex with her husband. Some women give birth only once and are unable to conceive another child in spite of their efforts. Internally, they feel what medical professionals cannot detect; their ability to reproduce is being manipulated by dark unseen forces.

16. Chronic Spiritual Blockage

These individuals find bible study and prayer a struggle. They sense that they are being mysteriously opposed from building a solid relationship with God. They experience obvious interruptions every time they try to commune with God. Thoughts of God not loving them or that He is not real often plague their mind from out of nowhere. There is an unjustifiable distrust of men and women of God. Their presence makes these individuals uncomfortable. Preventions seems to always get in the way when they decide to go to church. They hate deliverance ministers, have difficulty retaining God's word, and difficulty staying at one church for long. They keep experiencing church hurt, and are drawn to controlling ministries that suck them dry of money and energy. It is a strong possibility that they may have joined a cult in the past. These individuals may also notice that random people love to prophesy over them, with or without an invitation to do so.

17. Limbo Curse

This is a curse that prevents any noticeable movement in a person's life. Year after year their life remains the same. Their works yield them no fruit and seem pointless. Their efforts only sustain them but take them nowhere near elevation. They don't go backwards or forward, they remain in place. People suffering from this curse hold much promise and when they examine their lives, they are confused by their inability to make progress. They feel like they're running on the treadmill of life going absolutely nowhere.

18. Use Me Curse

This is a curse that attracts people to individuals with an assignment to drain them of their resources and virtues without ever blessing or committing to them in return. The user may approach the individual for a number of reasons which may or may not be limited to: money, sex, prayer, counsel and/or personal affirmation. They approach by night but deny the individual by day. They brag that the individual is beautiful, special, anointed, and gifted behind closed doors but never in the presence of those who can seemingly promote or prosper them. They pretend to befriend the individual while hosting hidden motives. Oftentimes, the motive is to sift them for ideas and strategy. The sentiments are never reciprocated and the victim begins to resent the user and ends the connection only to attract another of its kind.

19. Chronic Sabotage

The stench of the sabotage curse can often go undetected by everyone but the victim. This curse loves to nitpick at its targeted host by sending occurrence after occurrence of confusion, which is designed to sabotage the person's reputation and to kill their destiny. This person seems to always be named in a lawsuit, scandal, disagreement, and/or an unfavorable situation. What works for others never works for them. Struggle is attached to everything that they attempt. For the most part, the individual is the victim but their frequent involvement in confusion sabotages any chances of justice or vindication on their behalf. This person feels victimized, unheard and disrespected.

Be Encouraged

I encourage you not to allow your heart to become troubled if you see yourself in any of the above examples. With the right help, you can and will break free just as Jesus promised. The works of the enemy are no match for the power of God that is working within you! You best believe that the adversary is nervous that you are beginning to understand how he has been operating in your life. He is going to do whatever he can to discourage you from reading any further. He will attempt to incite fear within you. However, do you really think you have anything to fear based on what you have read so far? Hmmm, you already know!

Soul Work:

Given the signs of demonic oppression, which ones can you most relate to?

What emotions are you currently feeling and why?

Prayer:

Father, I see some areas of my life that are being affected directly by the enemy. Please help me.

Prayer Point:

Works of the enemy, you have no place in my life. Die by fire!

Chapter Terms: *Legalist:* spiritual rules without grace. **Bloodline:** *the families that you were born, adopted, and/or married into.* **Deliverance:** *the deliberate process of expelling demons from a person's body specifically through the power of Jesus Christ.*

(see Appendix A for covenant breaking prayers)

The Root of the Matter

Chapter 6

You do not have to say it, the signs of oppression listed in the previous chapter have you thinking really hard. I have been there, and experienced the same! I am quite sure that you were able to identify at least one area of your life where a curse could possibly be operating. If you are anything like I was, you are anxious and desperate to rid your life of the mess. I feel you. I remember where I was when I came to the realization that certain areas of my life were cursed. At the time, I was studying spiritual warfare but it was only at a surface level. I was upset because the new car that I purchased three weeks earlier was mysteriously damaged. It was the strangest thing! I walked into the house for a brief moment after washing it and when I returned, there was a dent on the hood that had not been there moments earlier. I looked around but saw no one. Heartbroken and confused, I began to cry. Later that day, I was mysteriously pushed down the stairs and hurt myself rather badly. A few days later, I discovered a bedbug infestation in my new home. I had to discard all of the bedroom furniture for both myself and my son.

Shortly thereafter, my supervisor left and it was falsely-apparent that my new supervisor had a strong dislike for me. A series of lost emails and text messages landed me in her office more times than I care to recall. I felt as if I was always defending myself against her. And to make matters worse, my efforts to provide proof that I had attempted to communicate with her were never enough. She verbally shredded everything that I did. I also noticed that many of my coworkers were unjustly monitoring and avoiding me. The enmity following my life was loud.

In the midst of it all, my position at work changed and I lost the monthly mileage checks that I depended on. The final blow came, when my program manager made the decision to transfer me to another unit even after someone else volunteered to go. I felt betrayed but I knew that God's hands were in the matter. Although I was a newcomer to spiritual warfare, considering everything that was going on, I knew enough to know that I was under spiritual attack. The accumulation of the events mentioned above did not happen by coincidence! There was a destiny fight taking place.

Thankfully, I did not take that season of my life personally. I saw it for what it was. The enemy was turning up the heat and God was using it to train me for what was to come. I was able to find peace because I looked at it from a spiritual perspective. I also knew that nothing I was experiencing would deflect God's love from me. With the enemy on my back, I transferred to the second floor as gracefully as I knew how. Although not in the natural, I perceived that changing positions was a promotion in the spirit realm. In fact, it later proved to be one of the best decisions ever made for me. I was literally propelled even further into my destiny. I worked with some of the most beautiful coworkers and clients alike. I later spoke with my former supervisor and found that she was just as perplexed by our brief time together. We laughed at what the enemy attempted to do and eventually became cordial.

Reader, I understand that life is not about perfection, and not everything will always go according to plan. However, I do believe, as I've already stated, I should win in every single situation because I am a child of God. I made the decision that I wanted to be like Jesus because there is no defeat in Him. When I first examined my life, all I saw was defeat, way too many setbacks, and a lot of delay. I saw negative patterns that seemed to laugh at my chances of attaining the prosperous future that God promised me. I did not see any evidence of those thoughts of good and not of evil as promised by God in Jeremiah

29:11. One day, I spoke with one of my second floor coworkers about my intuition. I shared that I felt as if I was cursed. I continued to do my research, and to my amazement, I saw my life! I cried out to God, "There are curses hanging over my life and I want them gone! God, will you help me?" Of course, my loving Savior responded, "You already know."

It was within a matter of seconds that this journey to break the very back of the enemy became serious business for me. Men and women of God, I know that you are fed up. I also know that you may be feeling anxious and ready to wage war on the enemy. However, it is not wise to go into battle ill-equipped. You must take a strategic stance when dealing with Satan. Before addressing and breaking curses, it is very important that you determine how you got into this position. The Bible states, "With all thy getting, get understanding" (Proverbs 4:7). Having an understanding will not only help you break free and remain free, it will help you identify the strongholds operating in the lives of others so that you can help them break free as well. Once you attain a certain level of freedom, helping others break free is your reasonable service. I told you how I came to the awareness that curses were attached to my life. Let's discuss what I learned pertaining to how they came about.

Someone Gave Your Bloodline Over

How much do you know about your family history, and how far back does your knowledge travel? I am not only talking about your immediate family. Your life is affected by at least six major family strands whose blood is flowing through your veins.

1. Your Mother and Father
2. Your Father's Maternal Bloodline and Your Father's Paternal Bloodline.
3. Your Mother's Maternal Bloodline and Your Mother's Paternal Bloodline

Spiritually speaking, if there are curses resting anywhere on the six strands of your bloodlines, those curses have a legal right to claim you by virtue of your DNA. In fact, I believe most of the demonic struggles we face in life have everything to do with our bloodline offenses, and very little to do with our personal offenses. Well, at least that was the case for me. Do not get me wrong, I take full responsibility for my cooperation in sin. However, I now know that bloodline demons were rising up and demanding a sin offering from me even before I knew what sin was. Unbeknownst to me, my participation in sin not only anchored their presence more securely in my life, it gave them the permission and access needed to freely steal, kill, and destroy at will. My early lifetime of ignorance and willing cooperation with sin placed not only myself but the life of my unborn son in danger. Even at this point in life, what I fail to deal with will confront him.

Even if you have a decent understanding of your family history, it is all surface information. You have no way of knowing the ins and outs of the private or public lives of your ancestors. Unless you are well informed, and there are many who are, you have no idea whether someone in your bloodline practiced witchcraft. If you do, I am certain that most do not know to what extent. There are some families that are very open regarding their involvement in witchcraft, although they may not openly call it that. I have lost count of the number of deliverance cases that I have encountered in which individuals found out that they, or their bloodline, had been given over to demons through the practice of witchcraft on the bloodline. The information was revealed as demons spoke out through them. It quickly became the norm for demons to manifest and proclaim that they had a legal right to remain in that person's body because of pacts, covenants, and oaths made on behalf of the bloodline.

In some instances, contractual terms were not made at all. Walking into the enemy's camp to utilize his services was all that was needed to capture the bloodline. For instance, speaking with a spiritualist about your life is one of many examples. When anyone goes into the enemy's camp, they aren't just representing themselves, they take their bloodline with them. Unfortunately, that's how some families get tied up. The more often the individual goes, the deeper the tie and the sacrificial requests. During various deliverances, demons boasted that human and animal sacrifices were made, while others communicated that money or a handshake was exchanged. Bloodlines are usually given over in exchange for protection, wealth, power, food, love, healing from sickness and disease, or for the sake of causing harm to a perceived enemy.

The stipulations surrounding demonic contracts vary, and are based on the demands of the entities in charge. I have noticed that agents of darkness usually target the wealth of a bloodline and wealth does not always equate to money. Nevertheless, such stipulations may have included that the women of the family would never get or stay married. Other stipulations may have included the attachment of poverty, strange illnesses, or negative happenings that follow the bloodline such as: short life spans, destiny blockages, or the requirement that witches and warlocks are raised up in order to continue their evil work. Please be advised that this is not an exhaustive list of stipulations. The demonic world is complex and the stipulations are various and plenteous.

Do not be so shocked! Think about it. Desperation and greed coupled with a lack of faith in God will drive a person to do just about anything. For example, suppose your great-great-grandmother was stricken with cancer and did not have access to healthcare. How easy would it have been for her to give all of the family women over to witches in exchange for the removal of the cancer from her cancer-stricken body? I'm here to tell you that it would not have been hard at all choosing between living and dying.

I recall walking a young Haitian lady through deliverance and it was revealed that she and her sisters had been given over by her father, who was a warlock. Did it matter to him at all that he was giving his daughters over to demons in exchange for money and power? Absolutely not! Unlike the grandmother mentioned above, the father knew exactly what he was doing and he made a willful decision to do it. Yes, the great-great-grandmother succumbed to desperation because of her situation. Little did she know, it was all a setup to secure her bloodline. She went to a witch doctor for help for a sickness that was possibly placed on her by agents of darkness in an effort to capture her business. Agents of darkness cannot heal. That's a Godly virtue. They can only reverse their own works. Due to spiritual ignorance and as a result of being allegedly healed, her faith was sealed in witchcraft. She became a faithful customer, and all of the destinies of the family's females had been sealed, unbeknownst to them. Not only that, her example introduced witchcraft as a norm to the bloodline.

The bottom line is this, the details as to WHY we seek demonic assistance do not matter because demons do not play fair. They understand spiritual laws regarding seeking information from the enemy's camp. Once they have established a contract on your behalf, they will continue to collect generation after generation unless they are stopped. And that is the job of a generational curse breaker. Our Father does not tolerate dipping and dabbling in the kingdom of evil. Consider the following scriptures that instruct against the pursuit of the "benefits" of the enemy:

Revelation 21:27 • Revelation 21:8 • Galatians 5:19-21 • Micah 5:11-12 • Micah 3:7 • 1 Samuel 15:23 • Leviticus 19:26 • Deuteronomy 18:10-13 • Revelation 18:23 • Isaiah 47:12-14 • Isaiah 8:19 • Leviticus 20:26-27 • I Chronicles 10:13-14 • Revelation 9:20-21 • 2 Chronicles 33:6 • Nahum 3:4-5.

Friendly Foe

Another way you can find yourself under a curse is by the hands of an undercover, jealous friend or family member who does not want to see you prosper. So, they visit a witch to have a spell cast on you that is designed to reverse whatever seems to be going well in your life. There are cases where they do not have to visit a witch for their seething jealousy and hatred of you to translate into witchcraft. This type of witchcraft is one of the many works of the flesh as outlined in Galatians 5:19-21. Demons can capitalize on the negative energy and words that are spoken into the atmosphere about your life, and use them as justification and authorization to steal, kill, and destroy from you. Be warned, they will do just that if you are living a life of compromise. A life of compromise means that your spiritual armor is breached. As written in Isaiah 59:2, sin separates us from God. This in turn, allows attacks and weapons formed against you to prosper. If weapons formed against you are prospering, there is a reason why.

Offense

I recall being at a deliverance conference where a young man manifested a spirit named Michael. As the deliverance session progressed, it was revealed that Michael was the name of the young man's brother, who was very much alive. Apparently the young man had stolen Michael's girlfriend several years prior. Although this young man had moved on with his life and married another woman, Michael had ought against him that he was holding on to with all of his might. The young man and his wife drove ten hours for deliverance because he had become extremely confused and they knew that it was spiritual. During the deliverance session, the spirit confessed that a strong spirit of confusion had been sent to block his mind and bury his glory. The witchcraft spirit refused to go until the deliverance minister walked the young man through the process of apologizing to Michael in the spirit realm.

It was at that same conference that I learned the potential harm of offending someone. Therefore, I was prepared when a spirit of witchcraft manifested through one of my students during a deliverance session I was conducting. It claimed that she was the spirit of the wife of a young man with whom the young woman was in contact. The spirit proclaimed that she had tried to harm the young lady several times, but all attempts had been blocked because of the young lady's prayer life. The witchcraft spirit communicated that the wife was jealous because her husband had feelings for the young lady and she wished those feelings were for her.

We all know that it is nearly impossible to go through life without offending someone. The downside is that you never know how a person will handle the offense. You have no control over his or her response. The offense magnify when the individual dwells on it and obsesses over it. This releases toxins that attract demons, and they in turn torment that person's mind with the offense. The spirits then use the will and words of the wounded to attack the offender. And as stated previously, if there is a breach in your spiritual armor, the weapons will prosper.

Crab Curse

The name of this curse is coined after the crab-in-the-bucket mentality. A crab curse is a curse that can be placed on you by anyone whose attention you attract with your success. In fact, there are cultures that are notorious for using the crab curse. When a person sees that you are excelling in some way, they haul themselves over to a voodoo priest, or whomever, in order to curse you. Anything that even resembles success can set them off. It could be your new job, boyfriend, car, house, pregnancy, your acceptance into college, skin color, hair type, body shape, personality, sense of fashion, or even your love for God. Their main mission is to keep you from prospering by any means necessary. One day everything is fine and the next day all hell breaks loose and you lose the blessing. Getting back on track is next to impossible without breaking the curse. Once again, these curses can only stick if there is a legal right in place. Otherwise, curses are powerless over you.

Sexual Violation

Sexual violation happens when a person is forced or manipulated to perform or endure sexual acts against his or her will. The violation serves as a sin offering. Being sexually violated on any level can open you up for demonic oppression. I know this makes absolutely no sense whatsoever because you did not ask for it to happen. Remember, demons do not play fair. It takes a demonized individual filled with sexual perversion, among other things, to violate another individual. Once the act is committed, spirits are transferred to you and/or your partner in addition to those spirits that were already claiming you.

Word Curses

Many people fail to understand the power of their words and how words stick to the soul. When God was ready to establish order in the earth realm, He spoke and it was so. Words are laced with energy and when they escape our lips into the atmosphere, they look for a place to rest, take root, grow, and yield fruit. A curse can take root in your life after escaping the lips of an individual who refused to taste their words first. One of the first steps that I walk an individual through during deliverance is the breaking of word curses. Thousands upon thousands of people meet defeat in certain areas of their lives because of the words that were spoken over them. These poison-laced words stick to their souls and haunt them in still moments. Some examples of word curses are as follows:

- You will never amount to anything.

- You are ugly and fat, and will always be.
- You act just like your no good father.
- You are a dumb little (expletive).
- You are good for nothing.
- Nothing will ever prosper for you.
- No manner of man or woman will ever desire you.

People do not realize that they are partnering with demons when negative words are spoken. They are literally giving demons permission to curse you. The demons then take those words and ensure that they take root and bear demonic fruit.

Guilty by Covenant or Association

Curses can also operate in your life when you are connected to a person who is cursed. For example, a man who handles money well marries a woman who has a poverty curse over her life. As a result, he discovers that money is leaving his life at an alarming rate. This is happening because the two are in a covenant relationship. Therefore, what is attached to her now has a right to attach itself to him.

Another prime example is a young lady who is living a chaste life, and befriends or dates someone who is filled with lust. Over time, the young lady begins to be tempted, and in some cases, attacked by suggestive thoughts of perversion that were not there prior to the friendship/relationship. The association draws the attention of thirsty demons. Spirits are polygamists, and the more people they can ensnare, the merrier they are.

People can also become cursed by knowingly or unknowingly entangling themselves with someone who is practicing witchcraft. This happens to many who sleep around. Far too many have had their destinies snatched by agents of darkness. As a result, their lives dry up to nothing over time. They can trace the blatant turn of events to the entry of that individual into their lives. No one taught them that whatever is attached to the people who have access to them, has the right to attack them.

Beloved, I admonish you not to be afraid, but to rise up in holy boldness and declare that you will no longer carry loads that do not belong to you. I can hear, once again, your heart asking, "Minister Faithe, this is a lot! Do I truly have the power to break free?" My response to you is, you already know!

Soul Work:

Do you believe that there is a curse hovering over your life?

If so, what do you believe is the origin of the curse?

Prayer:

God, I perceive that there is a curse hovering over my life and I want it gone.

Prayer Point:

Every curse hovering over my life, drown in the blood of Jesus.

Chapter Terms: *Root: tthe beginning stages of a live thing.* **Curse:** *the enforcing of demonic contracts and covenants.* **Deliverance Session:** *a formal meeting designed to walk a person through the process of casting demons from out of them.*

(see Appendix B for covenant breaking prayers)

Your Hand in the Matter

Chapter 7

The wonderful thing about God is that He left an awesome blueprint for us to live by. He is not spiritually double-minded, bipolar, or schizophrenic. God is consistent and His core values are always the same. He is a prevention strategist who does not mind getting His hands dirty in order to accomplish the job. He is powerful and all-knowing. He is very resourceful, and creates what He does not have access to. He is very detail-oriented. He thinks everything through, and every single decision He makes is perfect. In him, there is nothing lacking or missing. He is amazingly perfect.

Unfortunately, when a person does not know God, he or she does not trust nor follow Him. When a person does not trust the beauty and sovereignty of God, they tend to compromise and try to rearrange His established order according to what makes them feel good. This applies even to alleged born-again believers who live sub-par lives. They shout all over the church, speak in tongues, and throw money on the altar but their lives are raggedy behind closed doors. I distinctly remember having a desire to live holy. When I looked at the saints to whom I had access to. I observed that none were living a life worth modeling. Some had money and fantastic possessions, but they were lacking in the areas that mattered most to me. I remember innocently thinking, *"It must not be possible to live holy."* All I saw were so called Christians compromising. They rationalized what parts of God's word they would or would not accept. They took matters into their own hands by toying with the idea that God does not actually mean what He says. According to John 8:44 (NIV), Jesus had some very strong words to say about such individuals. He stated, "You belong to your father, the devil, and you want to carry out your father's desires. He was a murderer from the beginning, not holding to the truth, for there is no truth in him.

When he lies, he speaks his native language, for he is a liar and the father of lies."

If you are anything like me, you want God, through Jesus, to be your Father and not the devil. Examine your life. Examine your mindset. What doors have you opened for the enemy? It is now time for you to find your hand in the matter. Things are truly about to get sticky and I am excited for you. Now that you have a solid understanding of how others can impose curses on you, we will explore the doors you may have opened that invited demonic oppression into your life. As addressed earlier, this may have been done willfully or ignorantly.

1. **Open Doors**

Involvement in any of the following: Occult, Voodoo, root, witchcraft, black/white magic, visiting a spiritualist, Obeah, Santeria, visiting psychics and/or fortune tellers, and soothsayers are all offensive to, and forbidden, by God. You are automatically initiated into witchcraft when you partner with the enemy or go into his camp to obtain information. By doing so, you open yourself up for attacks. One day, you may decide to walk away from the practice, but you will never be completely free until the covenant is broken and the demons that have entered your body are cast out. There is no other way around it; the curse will still be active until you break it.

2. **Secret Societies**

Involvement in Freemasonry, fraternities, sororities, and Eastern Star is a big NO! These organizations all appear to be innocent, in nature, on the surface because of their focus on community service and scholarship opportunities. Many of them even claim to be Godly organizations, but they are only name-dropping. All sororities, fraternities, and secret societies are laced with witchcraft. Your participation alone, results in you being initiated into witchcraft. I realize that many will attempt to argue with me about this, but it is because they are not high enough on the organization's ladder to be exposed to the darkness resting at its core. Do your research.

3. Demonic Games and Activities

Other open doors of initiations include playing with Ouija Boards, levitation games, Yoga, séances, Tarot Card readings, Astrology, reading your horoscope, fascination with books about magic, engaging Spiritualists, reading demonic books, watching demonic movies, and Transcendental Meditation, etc.

4. Abortion

Aborting a baby is considered murder and as blood sacrifice by demons. Having an abortion provides a legal right for a demon to oppress a person in many ways.

5. Fornication

Regardless of what society promotes, sex before marriage is inappropriate in the eyes of God. A person's willful intention to transgress the law of God by committing fornication gives demons just one more excuse to steal, kill, and destroy in that person's life.

6. Sexual Perversion

This includes homosexuality, lesbianism, adultery, masturbation, pornography, incest, sexual toys, orgies, bestiality, exhibitionism, fetishism, pedophilia, masochism, and sadism. A sexual perversion stronghold can also surface as a person's inability to get enough sex.

7. Studying and Practicing False Religions

Demons can also enter when a person ventures outside the true realm of religion in order to study or practice a false religion. Religions that fall under this category are those that deny Jesus Christ as the only way to God. I once walked a young lady through deliverance who manifested a Muslim spirit. She later communicated that she used to argue religion with her Muslim brother and at one point studied the religion and considered converting.

8. Trauma

Trauma at any stage of life can open demonic doorways. Doors for demonic entry are opened because of the victim's vulnerability and wounded soul. This is how soul wounds are formed. This is not necessarily a door that you directly opened. Nonetheless, it was worth mentioning.

9. Drugs and Alcohol

Drugs and alcohol lower a person's inhibition, which leads them to make decisions that compromise their moral beliefs. Drug usage and/or excessive alcohol intake will surely serve as gateways to invited demonic entry.

10. The Devil's Entertainment

Music such as heavy metal, vulgar rap, and compromising R&B songs open the door for demonic oppression. Music and lyrics of these types do not glorify God. Unbeknownst to many, there are some artists who pray demonic prayers over their music, and spirits are evoked once the songs are played in your home, office, or car. Couple this with alcohol and drugs, and the atmosphere is set for a demonic playground. You must also be aware of artists giving acknowledgments to God. Just because your favorite artist acknowledges God does not mean that God acknowledges them. God would never cosign on lyrics that conflict with his teachings. It is time to do some soul searching, ask yourself if your favorite singer would be able to perform his or her song in the courts of heaven. If the answer is no, you already know.

"Finally, brothers and sisters, whatever is true, whatever is noble, whatever is right, whatever is pure, whatever is lovely, whatever is admirable—if anything is excellent or praiseworthy—think about such things" Philippians 4:8 (NIV).

11. The Devil's Items

You can have items in your home that invite the enemy in, such as demonic paintings and sculptures from different polytheistic countries/cultures, shrines dedicated to false gods/the dead, candles and incense used in satanic rituals, items that have been given to you by agents of darkness as a point of demonic contact, pornography, Ouija board, crystals, demonic jewelry (evil symbols) and clothing dedicated to evil entities.

12. Gossip

This is an area in which most people are guilty, but they do not consider it as a doorway through which demons can enter and oppress them. Gossiping is a form of witchcraft, and a partnership is formed with demons when you gossip about another person's life. You enter into agreement with demons by repeating, creating, or entertaining contaminated information regarding another person. Therefore, strongholds are established and/or reinforced in the person's life that is being gossiped about. Eventually, you open yourself up to reap that which you have sown.

Over the years, gossip has taken on more sophisticated forms such as reality TV, the news, gossip magazines, gossip websites, and gossip radio shows. It is simple: if it does not glorify God, then it glorifies his enemy.

Let us return to the story that I shared earlier about looking around and feeling as if it was impossible to win in life, even as a Christian. As I reflect on that experience, I realized that God must have been stirred up by my thoughts, and He took my seemingly factual thought as a challenge to correct me. It was as if He had something to prove to me. A short while later, was when I had the open vision of an angel drawing his sword, and declaring that my life was on display. Reader, I can now see that I was calling the enemy's crumbs blessings. Wow! Thank you God for saving me from myself!

As a servant of the Most High God, I know for a fact that God is proclaiming to you at this very moment that He is taking this season of your life very personally. Accept the Father's invitation, take a moment and let God know that you are ready to partner with Him. By the way, when God is ready to shift a person, it begins with information. Ah, yes! If you are pondering if this is why you are reading such a book, you already know!

Soul Work:

What open doors can you identify with?

Why did you open those doors?

Prayer:

Dear God, I acknowledge that I need more of you in my life. I see myself in the pages of this book, and I want to break free. I choose this day to partner with you. I accept your proclamation over my life to take this season of my life personally. Amen

Prayer Point:

Every evil door that I opened in my life, be closed by the hand of God.

Chapter Terms:

Witchcraft: *skilled works of the enemy sent to bend, tilt, manipulate, control and rule over your life.* **Demonic Gateways:** *entry and exit points that the enemy uses to come and go in a person's life.* **Renounced:** *To verbally disagree with covenants that were made with demonic powers on your behalf.*

No Thank You!

Chapter 8

While trying to decide what to entitle this chapter, I kept hearing "No thank you." I was initially confused and thrown off by the suggestion but it all began to make sense as I submitted to what I heard. This chapter is about the power of the spirit of rejection. Rejection, on any level, says, "no thank you" to a person's existence and efforts in the earth realm. What could be more damaging to your soul than to receive a big fat **"NO THANK YOU"** before you get started well in life? Yes, rejection painfully and viciously strikes a person's life as early and often as possible. That is exactly what happened to me, and more than likely to you.

Just as marijuana is referred to as the gateway drug that opens the way to the exploration of heavier drugs, so is rejection in the culture of deliverance. We refer to rejection as the gateway demon that opens the door to lower and higher ranking demons. As a deliverance minister, I have not met anyone who did not need deliverance from the spirit of rejection on some level. What amazes me about this spirit is that it is very easy to identify and cast out. When appropriately and forcefully addressed, rejection gives no opposition whatsoever. Like many of the other demons, rejection does not attempt to hide his presence or works. In the back of my mind, I wondered why.

During one particular deliverance service, a very weak sounding spirit of rejection manifested. Before casting it out, I commented on how weak it was and it responded, "I may be weak but the work that I do, and the stains I leave are powerful." Rejection's answer stunned me because I knew exactly what he meant. Getting the spirit to leave is the easy part. However, dismantling his works and erasing his residue is a very tedious process. It is such a tedious work because most of the battle takes place in a person's emotions, where the imprints of its works are stored. Rejection's mentality is, "Sure, you got me. I'll go because most don't have enough patience, endurance, or exposure to the tools necessary to uproot my works."

The Million Dollar Question

When exploring the results of a client's assessment, one of the first questions I whisper as I search for answers is, "Who rejected you?" Locating who did it and the details accompanying the rejection puts me in a better position to determine the driving factor behind a lot of their destructive decisions in life. This information also assists me in identifying what other demons may be present. I am confident that we all can agree that every single person on the face of the earth craves love and acceptance whether they want to admit it or not. A person can quote, "As long as I have King Jesus I don't need anybody else" all day long, but that is an absolute lie. It is one of those lies that no amount of fulfillment in Christ can erase.

No matter our place of origin, we are human beings living on Planet Earth. Just as oxygen and water are required to sustain life, love and acceptance are absolutely vital to a person's ability to thrive. We interact with our fellow humans every day. The Father created us to influence and inspire each other, and rightly so. In appropriate scenarios, we are, in essence, being influenced by and drawn to the God part of that individual. When the connection is good, it is actually God accepting and loving us through each other. We are designed to build up and encourage each other as we fight through our humanity on the path back to our birthplace, the throne of God.

The Family

There are vital institutions that God created that I believe were established for the added benefit of combating the spirit of rejection.

The family unit is one of those institutions. For instance, God proclaimed in Genesis 2:18,"It is not good that the man should be alone; I will make an help meet for him." In my opinion, this proclamation was more than some sentimental banter of love as many romantics suggests. Without trying to be a theologian, I will just settle the matter by saying, God considers and addresses all angles and scenarios before implementing decisions. Adam and Eve's union not only combated a need for companionship and Eros love, it presented a layer of protection against the arrows of rejection that were sure to travel their way curtesy of Satan and his crew. God understood very well what they were up against. Whenever rejection threatened their boarders, not only did they have God, they had each other for validation and affirmation. They could remind each other of their true identity in God. Even if the offense occurred at the home base, a loving apology was all that it took to minister to the pain and provide restoration.

Do you realize that Adam and Eve's fall did not take our all-knowing God by surprise? Even so, their act of rebellion against Him came with consequences that resulted in their eviction from the garden of Eden. Their disobedience led to a very painful "no thank you" sting from their creator. And let us not forget that Eve felt her first sting of "no thank you" from her husband when he blamed the entire ordeal of eating from the forbidden tree on her. The Father rejected Adam and Eve by withdrawing the free flowing access that they had to him. Prior to the fall, they walked and talked with Him daily. The God of the universe was their covering, coach, spiritual father, creator and so much more. However, just like what occurs in a bad breakup, when they crossed a God, access was denied. Don't feel bad for them. Rejoice because death was their reward and because of Jesus, they dodged the death-bullet. Trading in beauty for ashes, God allowed them to have each other. Just think what would have happened had Eve been the only person to sin. Of course Jesus would have died for her too. However, she would have had to leave the garden solo. She would not have had Adam's support and the darts of rejection would have given her a complete run for her "First Lady Of the Earth" anointing.

Even so, God could have separated them, but He did not because He understood the importance of forgiveness, unconditional love, and acceptance. In the face of betrayal, God kept the first family together. I believe family connectivity is designed to sustain us and to protect us from the cruel world of loneliness and rejection. Your family should be your safe place. They should be the people that provide you with the experience of safety and unconditional love. Unfortunately, this is not always the case.

Household Rejection

While teaching a class on spiritual warfare, the topic wandered over to rejection and why it seems to be at the core of all demonic entry and activity. The Lord began giving me some awesome revelation that expanded my level of understanding regarding the spirit of rejection. No one knows the pangs of rejection like God does. Did you know that the first outward display of sin in heaven showed up through rejection? Pride was found in Lucifer and it led him to reject God. What a devastating blow it must have been to the Kingdom of Light to experience such betrayal and rejection!

Lucifer was an anointed Cherubim who was also the angel of worship. His ministry surrounded the heart of heaven, and he was created to dwell eternally in the throne room of heaven, in the very presence of God (see Ezekiel 28:14). However, Lucifer essentially said "no thank you" to his creator, the God of the universe; the very embodiment of love, righteousness, grace, and perfection; your Father and my Father. The most destructive aspect of his behavior is that he did not leave his beef between him and God. He used his now sin-contaminated influence to persuade one-third of the heavenly host to abandon their allegiance to God and pledge it to him. They disgustingly echoed the cancerous sentiments of their newfound god, "no thank you." Some might foolishly brag that two-thirds of the heavenly host remained although one-third abandoned God. True. However, what they fail to understand is that the rejection of just one person of importance can send one's life spiraling out of control. It can cause an upset in ANY setting.

Please do not misinterpret my statement. I want you to understand that God was not affected by rejection the same way that Lucifer and his thugs were. The spirit of rejection devastated heaven because sin cannot stand in God's presence. God was indeed going to respond, and He did so by permanently ejecting the rejecter from heaven. It was all fun and games when Lucifer was on the giving side of rejection. He was in no shape, form or fashion ready to be on the receiving end; although it was him who threw the first rejection punch.

The ramifications of his actions resulted in his eternal separation from God, and landed him a death sentence. Talk about an ultimate blow of rejection! I cannot help but wonder if Lucifer ever imagined that God would actually reject him. Hmmmm, or did he think that God was going to negotiate his stay in heaven? Whatever his thought process, he was stabbed by God's rejection knife and is still feeling it to this very day. I choose to believe that he never meant for things to manifest as they did.

Satan and his thugs are reminded of God's rejection every time they see you lift your hands in worship; every time you call on God's name; every time you cry in God's arms. He feels the sting of rejection all over again because he wants what you have. However, it is absolutely too late for him. He hates the administration of the Holy Spirit and the way the angels of God serve you. He hates your access to God and does everything that he can to disrupt it. It is his life's mission to make you feel rejected. He also wants you to join him in hell's lake of fire which will be his grand finale.

Family Attack

Satan has, and continues to level his attacks on the family structure by weakening its foundation. One of the ways that he does this is by slipping rejection into the equation as early as possible. Think about it, his first taste of rejection began on his home turf so it makes sense for him to start in your home. Listed below are ways that the enemy uses rejection to create a breeding ground for demonic oppression in a person's life at an early age.

I encourage you to examine your life as you go through the list. Please take what you read very seriously. I will admit in advance that some of these examples sound sketchy, but I want you to keep in mind that anything that goes against God's intended order causes confusion in the spirit realm. I would like to add one more thing before we move forward, we have already discussed that spirits do not play fair. So, it should be of no surprise that they take seriously what we may consider to be minor or no big deal at all.

1. Absent Parent

Growing up without a father or mother introduces rejection into a person's soul no matter the circumstances. In many cases, the child is not given a detailed explanation of why the parent is not involved in his or her life. They wander through life filling in their own details and of course, demonic entities specialize in magnifying that void. The soul knows the difference even if a non-biological substitute fills the void. The absence of a parent, or both parents, leaves a soul wound that must be addressed in order for total healing to take place.

2. **Thoughts of Abortion**

Believe it or not, the mere act of entertaining the idea of an abortion can invite a spirit of rejection into a fetus's life. Many women entertain the thought of having an abortion when they simply do not want children, failed to use protection, already have too many children, became impregnated when violated, desire children but feel it is not a good time, and/or when they are pressured by their partner to abort. Regardless of the reason, it translates into rejection. This is part of my story. My mother considered aborting me because she could not be in nursing school while pregnant. I entered the world wearing a mark that attracted rejection to me. That was my story until that spirit was cast out of me.

3. **Being Passed Off to Relatives**

Although this is a common occurrence in many cultures, it translates into rejection and abandonment when children are raised by anyone other than their biological parent(s). The quality of love the child receives at the hand of a caregiver is not the issue; the issue has more to do with how the soul interprets the situation.

4. **Gender Disappointment**

The spirit of rejection entered many people because one or both parents were disappointed that they were not of the opposite gender. Daddy wanted a boy, but you were a girl. Mom desperately wanted a girl and was devastated when she found out you were a boy. I remember the devastating feeling I had when I found out I was pregnant with a boy instead of a girl. Since learning about the many ways that rejection attaches itself to a person's life, I have apologized to my son and broke the spirit of rejection from over his life.

5. One Sibling Preferred Over Another

We know from the story of Joseph, in the Bible, that when a parent prefers one child over the others, the non-preferred sibling feels rejected. There is nothing comforting about receiving a "No thank you," from either or both of your parents.

6. Overworked Parent(s)

Children can acquire a spirit of rejection from feeling neglected by overworked parents. Once again, the details of why the parent is busy are unimportant because it is all about how the soul interprets the situation. Demons dig into soul wounds in hopes of gaining entry. Do not approach this with your sophisticated adult mind by thinking that this idea is outlandish. Children internalize things and take them personally because their brains are not developed well enough to bargain and process facts. As a result, some children rationalize the absence of a working parent as an indication that something is wrong with them. A child may verbally express their understanding of why you missed all their important events, but it still does not fill the void felt by your absence. Neither does it change or lessen the pain felt when other parents are observed in positions of support for their children, and you are not there.

7. Negative Words

There is nothing more beautiful than receiving words of affirmation and blessings from your parents. Imagine the power of a parent saying to their child, "May the blessings of God fall upon you. May the God we serve, honor and favor you until your work on earth is done." How beautiful to hear from your parent's heart, "You are incredible and our love for you is unconditional. When you fall, it is okay. Get back up and keep going." Unfortunately, this is not the case for everyone.

As a social worker and an observer of humanity, I have witnessed parents calling their children names I dare not repeat. Many are speaking death over their children instead of speaking life. It is NEVER appropriate to verbally shame your children with profanity or word curses. When you do, you are rejecting them. You are partnering with demons by telling them their presence on earth is pointless. What you say or neglect to say to your child(ren) matters.

8. Physical Abuse

What better way to reject your child than to use his or her body as a punching bag. "Spare the rod, spoil the child" is a famous line parents use to justify brutal discipline of their children, and the enemy absolutely loves it. I was amazed by the number of parents who supported Adrian Peterson's brutal assault of his defenseless 4-year-old son when the boy pushed one of his siblings. After seeing the photos of the bruises, I was outraged and found myself in the middle of many debates regarding the matter.

Countless men and women argued that they received similar beatings while growing up and turned out just fine. They further expressed that the children of today have too many rights because their parents cannot freely discipline their children. I tried to present the position that brutal beatings are not behind their "success" in life. In fact, I believe that correction and time influences success. Furthermore, just because something did not kill you does not mean that it did not affect you. As Paul so beautifully articulated to the Corinthians, when we grow older, we mature and put away childish things (1 Corinthians 13:11).

Many African American parents do not see the connection between how they discipline their children and how the "Massa" disciplined our ancestors. They beat the hell out of them with any tool they deemed worthy enough to inflict the most pain. I am a former Child Abuse and

Neglect Investigator, and we never told parents they could not discipline their children. My job was to intervene in an effort to prevent the discipline from escalating into abuse, or to enforce protection when my involvement occurred after the fact.

As a child, I received brutal beatings at the hands of my father until my mother intervened. These beatings often left me bleeding from scratches and cuts on my delicate body. I was a child with childish ways. My father never verbally corrected me for my mistakes. He gave little instructions but was quick to swing the belt, switch, or extension cord. I was in no position to defend myself emotionally or physically. As a child, I felt undervalued and rejected by him. I felt that I could do nothing right, and that he took pleasure in beating me. I was convinced my father hated me. It was not until I grew older that I learned that he was only modeling behavior he had been taught. He has since apologized and all is well.

9. You Don't Speak My Language

Gary D. Chapman's book, The 5 Love Languages, put into words what many of us could not articulate. Mr. Chapman was able to identify five areas by which people express love: receiving gifts, quality time, words of affirmation, acts of service, and physical touch. When a child does not receive expressions of love in his or her love language, it can translate into feelings of rejection. The parent may be showing love to the best of their ability, but it does not translate into love for the child. They are speaking a love language the child does not understand. The enemy uses this to bring enmity between the child and the parent. The parent feels rejected, and so does the child.

For example, Mr. Brown is a very hard working man. His love language is receiving gifts. Therefore, he works a lot so that he can meet his many obligations and shower his family with gifts. All the members in the household share the same love language, except for little Tommy. When presented with a gift from his father, Tommy is dismissive of it. As a result, Mr. Brown is insulted and views Tommy as being ungrateful. A frustrated Tommy becomes offended by his father's assessment, and he does not know how to articulate what is intertwined into the fabric of his very existence; he desires quality time, not gifts. Both walk away feeling rejected.

10. Sexual Violation

Nothing, and I do mean nothing, makes a child feel more rejected than being sexually violated by a parent, sibling, or other family member. It is betrayal on an unprecedented level and yes, it translates into a big fat "no thank you." The child slides further into the boiling pot of abandonment and rejection when a non-participating parent or relative knows about the violation but does nothing about it. There are far too many reports of mothers trying to have a "Stella

Got Her Groove Back" moment and unknowingly invited sexual predators into their home. It is a sad, but true fact that many mothers become enraged and lash out at the child once they report the sexual abuse. In essence, they have just denied that child's truth. Cringe as you may, but this scenario is more common than you know. My experience as a social worker supports every sentence written on the matter. The breakdown of the family leaves a child vulnerable. It is very hard for the enemy to infiltrate to the extent that he would like when the family structure is tight, and God is at the center of the home.

The Million Dollar Question

People who are oppressed by rejection attract rejection everywhere they go. The spirit of rejection is so evil that it will purposely pair the victim with individuals whose spirits have the specific assignment of rejecting them. How is this done? The other individuals usually carry the spirit as well, and as you have already heard at one point or another:

kindred spirits attract. In this case, spirits attracts spirits. Reader, the spirit of rejection is a silent killer. If left unexposed and unaddressed, the cancer of rejection will attack and irritate every area of your life. How do I know? You already know!

Soul Work:

Who rejected you and how?

How has the rejection affected you throughout your life?

Prayer:

God, I have experienced a lot of rejection in life and it hurts. God, I do not desire to hurt anymore. Please help me.

Prayer Point:

In the name of Jesus, I command every trace of rejection to leave my body now!

Chapter Terms:

High Ranking Demons: *demons that hold more power than other demons.* **Foundation:** *the theories, principles, and actions by which you seek to build your life upon.*

(see Appendix C for rejection breaking prayer)

Unbreak My Heart, Untie My Soul

Chapter 9

Toni Braxton, a famed singer in the mid-1990s, released a song entitled "Unbreak My Heart." Although a very popular song, it reeks of a soul tie as it details the story of a woman agonizing over the death of her lover. Their romance was cut short when he was killed in a motorcycle accident. The song does not express whether or not the subject of the song was married to the woman. All we know is that she gave her heart to her man and the relationship ended tragically; thusly leaving her feeling devastated and abandoned. The amount of anguish that she experienced indicated that her soul was tied to him. Due to the devastation experienced by the abrupt ending of the relationship, her soul cried out through the agony, "unbreak my heart!" In other words, undo your damage.

Unfortunately, the lyrics describe the emotional state that thousands of men and women experience after a breakup not extending from death; although it may feel like death. I have been there. And such pain can only extend from a soul tie. Please do not misinterpret what I am saying as there is nothing wrong with mourning the loss of a relationship or person whom you love. What I am conveying is that when your soul becomes stuck and you cannot move on beyond mourning or missing that person within a reasonable timeframe, you're in trouble.

The majority of the messages I receive on my Facebook ministry page are from desperate young women asking for help breaking free from a soul tie. They often become frustrated with me when I do not offer a "churchy" response or a five-step solution. Instead, I encouraged them to take my assessment because soul ties can be complicated, and I choose not to hand out information that may not be applicable to the inquiring person.

What Is a Soul Tie?

A soul tie is the tying together of two souls in the spirit realm. Relationally speaking, this usually occurs through, but is not exclusive to, sex. Sometimes a soul tie can form through merely excessing over a person in your thoughts and/or spending quality time with a person. That would qualify strictly as an emotional soul tie. And yes, a person can have a soul tie with you and you not have one with them. Soul ties can be soulish, godly, demonic or a mixture of all.

When two people come together on a solid foundation, the bond can be beautiful. The union is void of knots and is considered healthy and godly. A solid foundation consists of both individuals being in an emotionally healthy state and one with God. They stand as individuals whose primary source of affirmation and validation comes from within and above. They see a relationship as an asset to their already fulfilled lives. When a soul tie is created on a cracked foundation, an entanglement is formed in the spirit realm that is filled with knots and as a result, a demonic soul tie is easily formed. A cracked foundation is one where an individual is not emotionally healthy and may also be dealing with some demonic strongholds. A relationship validates and affirms their emotional deficits.

Demonic soul ties alter a person's decision-making process and makes it difficult for them to fight for ending toxic relationships or simply moving on once a relationship dissolves. When a demonic or emotional soul tie is formed and one does try to break away, the soul tie keeps drawing them back in. Even if they manage to break free in the natural, their thoughts and desires still crave or are haunted by their former lover.

How Demons Benefit From a Soul Tie

Because the soul tie topic is so extensive, I am going to narrow it down to demonic soul ties that are formed through having sex outside of the will of God. With our best interest in mind, one of the reasons that God warned us to flee fornication is because of what forms in the spirit realm. Sex outside of marriage has the same spiritual implications as it does within the institution of marriage; it causes two souls to become one (Mark 10:8). When one participates in fornication, knots are formed in the soul because the bond formed is not spiritually legal. Remember, demons are legalists and opportunists; they capitalize on sinful behavior and use it as an excuse to keep people bound. In this case, they have a field day tying knots in the soul secured by unhealed areas of our lives. For example, it's easy for men and women with deep seated rejection and abandonment issues to fall into sexual sin and form a sexual and emotional soul tie with an equally unhealed individual. And instead of ending the unhealthy union, they hold on to each other or adopt an off again, on again status. Domestic violence, cheating, jealousy, verbal and emotional abuse are the variety of fruit found as a result of demonic soul ties. Sometimes it shows up through couples who marry and refuse to divorce even after the relationship dissolves. They may use money or convenience as an excuse to prolong the divorce. Truthfully, it's the soul tie because when a person is truly ready to break free, nothing can stop them. They will find a way.

Let us pretend that you were with Johnny for about three months and sex was involved. The relationship recently ended and you are devastated. Unbeknownst to you, Johnny took a piece of you with him when he decided to leave the relationship or the sexual arrangement and he left a piece of himself as well. Johnny is oblivious to the fact that he is carrying you and other women in his soul. The spirit of lust will not allow him to rest long enough for the Holy Spirit to arrest and purge him. He does not give much thought as to why he cannot settle down or why he keeps running back to exes, having sexual dreams, or why he cannot seem to satisfy his sexual cravings. This is happening because his soul is entangled.

Women manifest very similarly, but their soul ties are usually magnified by emotional torment. They cry, eat, revisit memories, stalk social media pages and conduct drive-bys. They even go as far as contacting his family members and adopting delusional ideas of reconciliation. Even when they move on in deed, their mind travels back and will drop their ideal guy at the drop of a hat to go back to their vomit. They will not break the behavior until the emotional wound is healed and the soul tie severed. A person can marry while hosting soul ties. And as a result, the unsuspecting spouse is married to a fragmented spouse and will never experience all of their spouse until the tie is broken.

What Does a Soul Tie Have to Do With Deliverance?

I chose to write about soul ties following the chapter on rejection because I believe they are kissing cousins, and are very relevant to deliverance. I am convinced that the spirit of rejection is at the core of ALL demonic soul ties, whether it is the fear of being rejected or a relationship brought together by the spirit of rejection. Attempting to administer deliverance without dealing with helping a person heal from rejection wounds and eradicate demonic soul ties can either prevent deliverance or leave a person with unaddressed demons.

Their Hideout

As with soul wounds, I have found that demons hide within the knots of entanglement of a soul tie and during deliverance, manifest as the knots are unraveled. Getting the person to walk through the process of breaking the soul tie is the real challenge. The emotional connection to the soul tie is so real that I have witnessed women of God walk away from deliverance because they did not want to end a toxic or adulterous relationship. Some sought deliverance because they were convinced it would make them more desirable to the man they were trying to keep or win back. I could share many stories of women who could not achieve their deliverance breakthrough until they renounced the soul tie between themselves and exes of long ago. Some women have even left my class after paying their hard earned money simply because they refused to divorce the thought that an old lover, who had obviously moved on, would eventually come back for them.

Thankfully, most of my experiences with soul ties were with women who had moved on in the natural but their souls remained stuck on that one person no matter how hard they tried to break free. After being walked through the required steps of breaking soul ties, they finally received their freedom—which seemed impossible prior to. I would also like to add that a soul tie with an individual can show up in a person's inability to forgive a former lover. Subconsciously they fear forgiving the person because unforgiveness is their only tie to them.

It's All About the Why

My role as a deliverance minister and inner healing therapist is not to focus primarily on the soul tie or how it was formed, but rather on WHY it formed. I believe in getting to the root of the matter. A soul tie is the result of a much deeper, foundational problem. In my professional experience, one must first understand a person's "why" in order to truly help him or her break free from a soul tie. Everyone's "why" might be similar, but they are rarely ever the same. I am looking forward to sharing more on the subject in my next book, *Love On Your Rank In God... trade in your cross for your crown*.

If this chapter stirred your heart and there are tears rolling down your cheeks, you are probably wondering if your feelings for a certain person labeled as "love" are actually a soul tie being fueled by rejection. Be honest with yourself. Sweetie, if left unaddressed, the soul tie will complete its assignment of keeping you stagnant and unable to connect with or fully give yourself to your God-ordained spouse. In the spirit realm, you are bound to someone else. All of your life you have been taught to avoid getting pregnant or contracting a sexually transmitted disease, but no one has ever addressed the seriousness of forming a demonic soul tie. I recently read a meme that truly blessed me and it reads as follows, "You think celibacy is hard? Try breaking a soul tie." Men and women of God, stop crying, "unbreak my heart!" because it is time for you to cry "untie my soul!" Could it be that you have not been able to shake your ex-lover because you are carrying the load of their soul? Hmm, you already know!

Soul Work:

Do you currently have a soul tie with someone?

How did the soul tie form?

How is the soul tie affecting your life?

Prayer:

Father, I acknowledge that I have an un-Godly soul tie and it is my desire for it to be unraveled.

Prayer Point:

In the name of Jesus, I command the soul tie to be unraveled and combusted by Holy Ghost fire.

Chapter Terms:

Cracked Foundation: *a foundation containing demonic roots* (see Appendix C for soul tie breaking prayer)

The Holes in My Soul

Chapter 10

Exhausted from a long day, I hurried to the telephone so I would not miss my last appointment of the day. The voice on the other end was chipper and full of strength. She was excited about the call to the point that I almost felt condemned for being tired. What stood out most was the young lady's confidence and how educated she was regarding spiritual warfare. Had I allowed, she would have taken over the assessment process. To the untrained ear, this session would have seemed quite easy. However, I know that no one contacts me just because. The individuals who make contact do so because God specifically led them to me so that they can be set free.

I will admit that the young lady's case was perplexing. She was part of a strong deliverance ministry at her church, and was well versed on the ins and outs of deliverance. She stated that she had previously walked through several rounds of deliverance (at her church) but could not attain total freedom from demonic oppression. She loved God and lived a life that pleased Him. She was happily married with three children and was a successful business owner. She wanted for nothing. However, she suffered from chronic feelings of rejection, jealousy, envy, and hatred. After reading her assessment and discussing the results with her, I found no open doors and no obvious legal rights. Instead of writing her off as an attention seeker, I sat silently waiting for the Holy Spirit to reveal that which was hidden, as is my custom.

My tiredness suddenly vanished as excitement took over. The teacher and revealer of all things was about to school me! I could tell that my silence was making my once chipper and confident client uncomfortable. However, she said not a word. From out of nowhere, the Holy Spirit spoke, "Her mother." So I repeated what I heard in the calmest voice I could muster, "It's your mother." Before I could say another word, she snapped, "Most certainly not! My relationship with my mother was rocky, but through the grace of God I've forgiven her, and we are the best of friends."

To provide a little history, the woman of God's mother was so consumed with a drug and alcohol addiction that she abandoned her daughter at the age of three. This poor child was left at home alone without any food or water. It was by the grace of God that a neighbor heard her crying and called law enforcement. Child Protective Services were called and upon their arrival, she was taken into their care until a relative could be located. She was eventually placed with her grandmother, who raised her until she graduated from high school. I had no reason to doubt that this woman of God had indeed forgiven her mother; but I could hear what she could not and that was the pain in her voice. I heard the giant defense mechanism roar in her voice, while the alarms sounded loudly in the spirit realm, "This is my hurting place!" This woman of God offered proof that she was not operating from a place of unforgiveness. I knew exactly where she was coming from. She did not want to hurt God nor admit to the possibility that she was walking around in deception.

As soon as I could get a word in, I whispered, "You have forgiven her and you do love her." I instantly heard a big sigh of relief, but I did not stop there. "You have indeed forgiven her, but the hurt and pain is still there. Your soul is filled with holes. Your soul is still hurting from what happened to you. You're trying to lead as normal a life as possible but when your mother abandoned you; your soul man took several punches that left holes that have yet to heal. For many years unforgiveness kept the holes from healing. When you came to Christ, you covered them up with forgiveness, but you never cleansed the holes to empty them of all the infection. What happened to you at the age of three was painful and devastating to your soul, and it is time to give your soul permission to acknowledge the hurt and heal from the root up. What happened to you is not okay."

All of a sudden, the woman of God began sobbing uncontrollably. These were no ordinary sobs; they were soul sobs embedded with much pain. They had been trapped in her body for thirty-seven years, and now was their moment of escape. Through the sobs rose the fragile voice of a little girl begging for help. This voice stated that she was alone and afraid. She further communicated that her mother had left her without any toys or food. Although caught off guard by what I was hearing, I recognized that the exposing of her soul holes demanded the manifestation of her fragmented soul. A fragmented soul forms when the soul splits at the time of a traumatic event, thusly creating at least two separate identities. The soul splits in order to protect and cope. Psychologists and clinical social workers call it dissociative disorder. You may know it as split personality. In this case, her three year old self clung to the pain and vowed to protect her. The woman of God was trying to live a gratifying life as an adult with an undetected, traumatized little girl living inside of her. I walked her through the lengthy process of merging the fragmented soul and healing the holes in her soul. After doing so, I addressed the strongman who just happened to be a principality demon named, Jezebel.

This cocky, arrogant demon was not pleased to be discovered. She bragged that she hid behind this woman's fragmented soul and had the most fun stabbing the holes. Jezebel's wicked confession included taking credit for tormenting this woman's mind with rejection, jealousy, envy, and hatred. Jezebel exclaimed, "She's no good for the kingdom; she's too bound. She's mine. I'm not going anywhere because I own her." Not fazed by Jezebel's rant, I sent the fire of God to her and every lower-ranking demon housed in this woman and demanded their exit; and just like that, the woman of God was set free.

I chose to address holes in the soul by telling a story that shows just how important it is to thoroughly address places of trauma. If left unaddressed, trauma can block a person's deliverance and the quality of their everyday life. This is especially true for Christians because we are taught to ignore our truth and our pain. We are taught to slap some Jesus salve on it and all is well. Not so! No matter who you are, it is important to process through your pain to a place of peace through Jesus Christ.

This woman of God had two major issues, a fragmented soul and soul holes. Please understand that not everyone who has soul holes has a fragmented soul. I have since observed that a fragmented soul will block deliverance. Soul holes do not necessarily block a person's deliverance, but they mostly cause the person to question the success of the deliverance because he or she continues to struggle with certain feelings and emotions at the most inopportune times. Are you wondering how? Well, I will tell you.

A demon does not have to reside in you to affect you. Demons cannot get back in once you are delivered. However, they are attracted to the stench of infected soul holes, and they do any and everything they can to irritate the wound. They will cause others to say and do things just to get a reaction from you. They will whisper painful sentiments that play into the wound until your reaction opens the door for reentry. Or, as in the case of the woman of God, the strongman never leaves and keeps opening the door for other demons to re-enter. If you have ever experienced trauma on any level and have never walked to a place of healing, you have soul holes that need to be addressed. Addressing soul holes is a process that requires honesty, transparency, and patience. It is not only essential for you to become free, but mandatory that you protect your deliverance so that you can remain free. I can hear you in the spirit saying, "Man, this deliverance process is no joke!" My response to that is, "Ha! You already know."

Soul Work:

What are the major traumas that you have experienced?

Who are the people that you are having a hard time forgiving?

Prayer:

Father, I acknowledge that my soul needs to heal from pains of the past. Please expose these areas.

Prayer Point:

In the name of Jesus, I command my soul wounds to expose themselves and be healed by the blood of Jesus!

(see Appendix C for soul wounds and trauma prayers)

Spiritual Sex Trafficking

Chapter 11

Did you know that God is very concerned about the marital destinies of His sons and daughters? Your cries ascending to his throne expressing your longing to become one with another, rest, He is, indeed, listening. As a matter of fact, God wants you to know that not only has He heard your request, He has already answered you. He admonished me to remind you that your desire to get married originated from His heart. Therefore, it truly honors Him to honor himself by putting a beautiful smile on your face and heart.

Yes, I can hear you complaining about being in prayer for a long time but nothing seems to be breaking but your heart. You cannot figure out why you are still single or why you are experiencing such difficulty staying in a lasting relationship. The only thing that makes sense to you is that God has decided that marriage is not your portion. Nonsense! There are many possible contributing factors as to why a person cannot break through to their marital destiny. I will give you a few examples: soul ties with former lovers, immaturity, poor body image/hygiene, unresolved emotional issues, instability, and divine timing are also to be weighed and explored. However, the least factor to be considered is the reality that hosts of unsuspecting men and women of God are involved in Spiritual Sex Trafficking.

Spiritual Sex Trafficking is a term that I coined in my pursuit to describe the involuntary sexual hijacking of a person by demons in the spirit realm. These demons claim the person as their spouse or lover and turn them into their sex slave. They have sex with the person in their dreams, while they are awake, or while they are drifting into a dreamlike state. They work very hard to keep the individual single or frustrated with their partners, whether in a relationship or marriage.

These demons can be referred to as spiritual spouses who take their orders by their governing demons, Incubus and Succubus. In Latin, Incubus means to lie upon and Succubus means to lie under. Incubus is the demon that descends upon the female and Succubus is the demon that descends upon the male.

Do Demons Have Sexual Organs?

I cannot answer that question with certainty, and neither can anyone else. If we were to consider this question from a functional point of view, then I would have to conclude that angels of God do not marry nor, to the best of my knowledge, do they reproduce (Matthew 22:30). Honestly, the issue is not debate worthy. However, we do know that fallen angels can transform into whatever form they desire, including angels of light (2 Corinthians 11:14). Therefore, they can manifest sexual organs if need be.

Do Demons Judge Beauty?

Demons have distinct personalities and can, indeed, judge beauty as indicated in the Bible:

When human beings began to increase in number on the earth and daughters were born to them, the sons of God saw that the daughters of humans were beautiful, and they married any of them they chose… The Nephilim were on the earth in those days—and also afterward—when the sons of God went to the daughters of humans and had children by them. They were the heroes of old, men of renown. Genesis 6:1-2, 4 (NIV)

Where Do Spirit Spouses Come From?

Many credible Bible scholars agree that the sons of God were indeed angels on assignment in the earth realm who decided to forsake their assignment. They ventured to marry the beautiful daughters of men. It's not that they were in love because darkness doesn't know love. When they aborted their assignment, as free agents, they were turned over to darkness. As if sin wasn't enough, they further diluted and polluted the bloodlines/DNA of the women they married. Children were born to these unions. And as a result, the Nephilim race was created. A Nephilim is a half-human, half-spirit being. The way that they were able to reproduce is tied to very dark works of evil and that is why their offspring existed with such supernatural powers.

What Was Their Mission?

These rebellious angels, once outside of God's counsel, made it their mission to instruct humanity on how to tap into the supernatural outside of God. Think of it this way, they taught humanity how to break into cars and hot wire them versus legally obtaining permission and gaining access utilizing the correct methods, keys. They were the FIRST to push the WOKE agenda. They were the FIRST to instruct humanity regarding their third eye. Earth's first occultists, spiritualists, witches and warlocks were trained and established by fallen angels. They pushed a polytheistic society. Among other dark acts, they taught humanity the mysteries that are embedded in the elements of the earth; including the solar system. Because they are void of light, they pervert everything that they touch.

The Flood Displaced Them

We have already established that a Nephilim is a half-breed supernatural human. Prior to the flood, the word of God tells us that humanity was out of control. Things were so bad that every imagination and thought of man was evil (Gen 6:5). Thankfully, God found a family who honored him and he asked the patriarch, Noah, to build an Ark in preparation for the catastrophic flood that he was sending to cleanse the earth. Everything not on the ark, at the appointed time, would die (Gen 6:7-9).

As you may well know, spirits cannot die. Therefore, their human bodies were destroyed during the flood but their spirits were not. As a result, they became disembodied spirits. I am one who subscribes to the thought that demons are different from fallen angels. I along with other Bible scholars believe that demons are actually the disembodied Nephilim spirits from the flood. There is the Incubus, Succubus sect that specializes in continuing the perverted practices of "marrying" humans that was first introduced by their ancestors. They seek men and women whom they can attach to spiritually and claim as their bride or groom. These spirits are trying to counterfeit an institution that does not belong to them, marriage. And yes, in the realm of the spirit, they are able to procreate with the subjects of their affection thusly producing what is known as, spirit children; spawns of Satan.

What Is Their Goal?

These spirits are trying to counterfeit an institution that does not belong to them, marriage. Demons need a place of habitation and your body provides that. Until evicted, they will use your body as a base of operation to carry out their dirty deeds. Their ultimate goal is to defile and snuff out God's glory in the subject of their affection, you. They desire to plant seeds of spiritual perversion that will take root in your mind, body, will, and emotions. When you are defiled spiritually, you stand tainted in the eyes of God. When you are defiled, the demons can rightfully build an accusatory case against you in heaven, thus blocking your blessings. They do not have true romantic feelings for you. They marry a person in the realm of the spirit and show their "love" by becoming possessive and killing everything good that's attached to them. When these spirits attach to your life, they are stealing, killing and destroying in one manner or another.

Where Is God In All of This?

As a descendant of slaves, I think back to the many examples of unions between black men and women that were interrupted by their masters. These men proudly wedded the women of their affection only to have their union tarnished as their owners raped and mishandled their brides because they felt they had a legal right to do so. The slave women were the slave owner's property, so what were their husbands to do? They had power but no authority to use it. There was nothing they could do. They had to watch helplessly and in humiliation as their beautiful brides were violated repeatedly at the master's choosing.

Similarly, this is exactly what our Father experiences when he watches His bride, the church (2 Corinthians 11:2) being raped and molested by demons. His sovereign hands are tied because of legal rights that will later be discussed. To be honest, this is why so many of you are becoming frustrated with God when you do not get the results you seek when you are shouting, speaking in tongues, praying, and fasting. In the meantime, demons are laughing and winking at your creator because they know the truth; you are unqualified to be rescued because you are spiritually contaminated. And even if you are living right in the natural, your demon husband/wife is working overtime to ruin your reputation in the realm of the spirit. They do this every time that they defile you. Sin separates from us from God whether it's committed in the natural or spirit.

What Gives Them the Right?

As you can see, legal rights are everything in the spirit realm and this is the part that so many well-meaning Christians miss. Every demon has a specific task of torment. They are not confused about their assignment. In the case of Incubus and Succubus, they are attracted to the stench of sexual sin and lust and that's their way in. I separated the two purposely because the Holy Spirit asked me to make the distinction that a person can be celibate and still be lustful. I will explain later.

At this point, I need to address the ways these spirits lay claim to their unsuspecting targets or bloodlines. One way they can enter is through evil bloodline dedications or perpetual bloodline perversion. The SAME SPIRIT can rape all of the women and men in the family for generations until eradicated. I once ministered deliverance to a young woman who disclosed that the same demon was sleeping with all the women in her family. No one realized it until she made mention of spirit spouses in a casual conversation while at a family function. All of the women involved in the conversation thought that they were the only ones suffering from the brutal sexual dreams and strange entity tracking them in their dreams. Upon further inspection, she and her relatives realized that none of the women in her family ever successfully married. Needless to say, her deliverance was powerful! As a matter of fact, the demon cried and begged to stay because in his sick mind, she was his wife and he truly believed that he owned her and that she could not succeed without him. He also confessed that he owned the bloodline and would not release the others.

Demons jump at the opportunity to inhabit a person's body when they have a special interest in them. They are attracted to the smell of sexual sin of any kind. At that point, they become intimate with the person (usually through dreams) and claim them as their spouse. They put a wedding ring on them in the spirit realm. Believe it or not, they create marital contracts with their lover's name written on it. When fighting a person's marital destiny before a God, they provided documentation and your sexual sin track record as justification to delay, hinder or down right BLOCK your marital destiny. MY GOD! This goes for both men and women. Listed below are the types of sexual sins that invite the demons in:

1. **Sexual Sin:**

Fornication, pornography, masturbation, and lustful thoughts.

2. **Sexual Perversion:**

Group sex, sex toys, bestiality, adultery, promiscuity, homosexuality, lesbianism, incest, sex chat rooms, sex phone lines, and prostitution.

3. **Sexual Violation:**

Molestation and rape extends an unintentional invitation to demons. Demons do not weigh details because they play dirty. Although the act was nonconsensual, the stench of sin attracts them and they seize the opportunity.

4. **Lustful Demeanor:**

There are saints who believe that they are not contaminated because they are not physically having sex. However, they think about sex constantly and are very flirtatious. Their conversations are laced with sexual innuendos. When they meet a person, they talk about what they would love to do to that person if they were not saved. Some even resort to masturbation and/or sex toys for satisfaction not realizing that it takes perverted thoughts to get aroused. They also don't weigh that while they are pleasuring themselves, they are performing for an invisible demonic audience. Others draw the line at fondling, passionate kissing, and/or dry humping. In their mind, they feel justified because it's not like they actually had sex because there was no penetration. Nonsense! They take sexy selfies that send subliminal messages of lust. They feast on TV shows promoting lifestyles that contradict sexual purity. These same men and women can also be observed wearing attire that incites lust. Ladies, this attire comment is not only for you as there are men who know that the imprint of their goods can be scoped through their tight pants. Sister saved-girl beats her face and adds hair and jewelry that says, "I am not proud of the original version of me." They gravitate toward certain perfumes and colognes because the pheromones attract humans who have a lust spirit. Unbeknownst to men and women alike, the stench of lust invites and secures spiritual marriages.

How Do They Appear?

In the Western world, spirit spouses primarily reveal themselves in a person's dreams. They present themselves to the individual as anyone they would feel comfortable with, such as a former or current lover, their spouse, someone they know, someone they are interested in, a complete stranger, a faceless person, or simply, as themselves. Besides having sex with a person in their dreams, spirit spouses can cause a person to awaken so aroused that they seek sexual relief.

They can even cause a person to orgasm in their sleep. As stated earlier, these demons can also descend upon a person while they are wide awake or drifting into a dreamlike state. They are agents of lust and can arouse a person so strongly that they stop WHATEVER they are doing in order to masturbate or have sex. Be mindful that I am not talking about natural desires, but those that are unnatural. This drive is so strong that it demands a course of action that will not accept no as an answer. For a Christian, the experiences may be quite pleasurable but short lived because of the condemnation, guilt, and shame that follows.

However, a run-in with a spiritual spouse is not always "pleasurable." Some men and women have reported waking up in pain as if they have had very painful sex. There has also been reports of people finding traces of sexual fluids present when they have not had sex with anyone; well that is, not with anyone in the natural world. Others have even found marks and bruises around their thighs and inner parts. Additional signs that a person may have a spirit spouse besides having sex in their dreams include: having dreams of getting married to an unknown person, swimming in the sea, nursing a baby, or seeing themselves in the ocean with people they do not know. Hopefully, now you can clearly see why not being able to recall your dreams is dangerous.

Reader, please be advised that you may start having dreams about these spirits because of this newly acquired knowledge. Stop! Do not blame the book for this. These entities have always been present but hidden. Your acquiring of this knowledge will forced them to reveal themselves in a more blatant manner. I do not want you to panic, instead, rejoice because they have been exposed and can be dealt with accordingly.

Are You In Shock?

I know what you are reading is blowing your mind because you can relate. I am not here to convince you that what I have written so far is true. I know that it is. I have walked hundreds of men and women of God through the process of evicting these spirits. The spirit of lust is wicked, and it is nothing to play with. God led me to this information after I cried out, "What's wrong with me?" No one told me about spiritual sex trafficking (SST). When I began reading about the fruit of SST, I began trembling and crying like a baby because I knew I had found the answer to why I had lost several boyfriends, and experienced a broken marriage and engagement.

At one point, I was a slave to sexual sin and a victim of SST. Incubus and Succubus are what we call marine kingdom demons, better known as water spirits. I had no idea this kingdom even existed, and that it had already decided that I would never break into my marital or spiritual destinies. I was baffled as to why nothing worked for me without serious prayer until I was led to this information. Incubus was blocking me and now I am blocking him! Thank you Jesus!

On the day of my wedding, a tropical storm ruined the church and reception sites where I was supposed to get married and celebrate at in Charleston, South Carolina. The sprinklers went off in one of the rooms where my bridesmaids were getting dressed. To top it off, my aunt's dress caught on fire during the ceremony. I was surrounded by so much conflict before and after the wedding that I became bitter. I had refrained from having sex with my husband until our wedding night, so I was excited about consummating our vows. However, I was quickly disappointed because what was supposed to be beautiful lovemaking caused me pain and this continued throughout the entire marriage. As a matter of fact, our marriage was filled with unexplainable conflict. Even my pregnancy was painful. I was bedridden for the first four months and the pregnancy ended with a C-section. My spirit spouse fought hard to abort to press me to abort my son. In order to ease my pain, he reasoned that a second abortion would not hurt since I had already had one.

The bedroom struggles and interactive conflict caused by my spirit husband drove me to look for answers from family members, friends, and a counselor. Their inability to provide the solution necessary to ease my troubled mind made it easier for what was already claiming my life to spring forth . I was eventually driven to find comfort in the arms and bed of another man. I can hear someone thinking, "This is bull!" Ha! You are thinking like that because you are looking around and you see so many women who seem happily married and they surely did not do it God's way. Yup! I understand because I used to think like that too. However, a marriage does not equate to heaven saying, "I Do" when the couple does. And it definitely does not mean that the marriage is free from sexual perversion and lust.

My girlfriend Jamonica and I were discussing an ex-lover, who by his own admission, admitted that he is unhappily married. Poor thang is trying his hardest to promote that he is. She made such a profound statement when she said, "He's doing it for the sake of his image and political aspirations." I asked her if she regretted not being with him and she said, "No." She went on to communicate, "Faithe, anything can look and sound believable with the right words and picture attached. I am one of the few who truly knows the truth." Her perspective blessed me, and this simple exchange resulted in an eye-opening revelation. Do you realize that many people's destinies will never materialize because they are connected to the wrong person? I know from looking at my life that to whom much is given, much is required. It is a proven fact that the enemy fights you in the place of your greatest influence. I am powerful by myself, but can you imagine what will happen when I connect with my ONE? Reader, sober up! Do not be so thirsty to change your last name that you fail to examine not only your bloodline, but his. Do not be so desperate to rock a ring because you feel that it is the upgrade that you need.

On the surface, there are thousands of beautiful godly marriages in the world. However, you do not know what price they paid or what they endured on the way to the altar. You definitely do not know what is going on behind closed doors and you do not know what they will face later that is designed to test the validity of their marriage. Perhaps it was much easier for your friend to get married because her marriage does not pose a threat to the kingdom of darkness like yours will. Maybe it was just her time, who knows? It truly does not matter because your focus should be on moving with the flow of God.

For those of you who are already in a marriage that leaves much to be desired, I want to encourage you. If both parties are willing, God can minister to your cracked foundation. Famed gospel singer, Tina Campbell and her husband, famed gospel drummer and singer, Teddy

Campbell are incredible examples of God healing a cracked marital foundation and creating something incredible and beautiful.

Now that we have gotten that out of the way; let us get back to the matter at hand. Walk with me and let us explore the following list of spirit spouse fruit.

1. Inability to maintain a stable relationship

Every relationship ends in disappointment no matter how promising.

2. Late marriages

These are men and women who break into their marital destiny in their later years after much struggle earlier in life. And when they do, they aren't as excited.

3. Prolonged engagements

You have a ring but cannot seem to get around to setting a date. There is always a reason why you cannot press forward; money is usually the excuse.

4. Blocked promotions and advancements

These spirits affect every aspect of your life. They do not want to see you prosper.

5. Fibroids

These tumors are planted in the target's body to cause barrenness or pain.

6. Painful menstruation

Women have very painful menses accompanied by prolonged and excessive bleeding.

7. Broken engagements

Just when the couple is celebrating, some mysterious wind breaks the engagement.

8. Infertility issues

These types of issues are caused in order to inflict worry and shame on the woman.

9. Bizarre Marital Conflict

Spouses find it difficult to get along with each other. Unjust criticism of their mate causes so much conflict that it leads to divorce. These spirits are very jealous. They literally claim their victim as their spouse. In their minds, they are married to them and specialize in bringing discord between them and their lover.

10. Low sperm count, erectile dysfunction, premature ejaculation
11. Painful sexual intercourse
12. Barrenness

The woman's womb is blocked by demonic forces so that she is unable to reproduce.

13. Inability to break into marital destiny or committed relationship, but no problem producing children
14. Painful pregnancy

Spirit spouses can cause pregnancy complications with the intent of discouraging the woman from ever giving birth again.

15. **Hormonal imbalances**
16. **Sexual addictions to pornography and/or masturbation**

One indulges even when his or her heart is convicted to avoid such.

17. **Sexual immorality, such as adultery**

They are in so deep that their affection toward their spouse is gone.

18. **Dreams of being given a ring or wearing a ring**

This signifies that you have been entered into a marital covenant with the spirit spouse.

19. **Blocked orgasms**
20. **Nightmares**

These spirits use nightmares to incite fear because fearful people seek comfort, and sexual immorality is always there to answer the call.

The Bottom Line

Spirit spouses are relentless, and deliverance is the answer to dealing with them. Once delivered, the person must purify their temple and flee sexual sin, or these spirits will come back. They especially love to creep back during ovulation when the female body naturally craves sex. Another point of reentry happens when a person is lonely, emotionally vulnerable, or during those times when they are at odds with their significant other. It only takes one moment of vulnerability for them to reinvade their previous host's body. In fact, a person's love for God has to be their motivation for maintaining a clean temple, not their desire for a spouse. I will not say that eradicating a person's spirit spouse will cause their God-ordained spouse to manifest overnight, because they still have to be processed and renewed in their mind. However, walking through deliverance will clear the path for his or her arrival. Chains of lust will break and fall off, and they will experience freedom and a sound mind. They will begin to win in every area of their life in which they were previously bound.

When I began writing this chapter, I had no intention of sharing so much of my life with you. Hopefully, my transparency will inspire you to own your truth with the assurance that there is victory on the other side if you faint not. No demon has the right to invade and claim a body for which the Lord Jesus Christ died and rose again! Do you believe that our father is ok with you being a victim of SST? You Already Know!

Soul Work:

Do you see the workings of spiritual sex trafficking in your life? If yes, in what areas?

What do you believe exposed you to the spirit spouse?

Prayer:

Heavenly Father, I repent for all of my sexual misconduct. Please forgive me and cleanse my soul.

Prayer Point:

In the Mighty name of Jesus, I issue any spirit who is claiming me as its bride or groom a divorce decree.

(see Appendix C for spirit spouse and sexual perversion breaking prayers)

Suffer Not a Witch to Live

Chapter 12

Here I am, days away from being completely done with my book and the Holy Spirit instructs me to write an entire chapter on witchcraft. I knew that this area needed to be addressed but I was trying to avoid it. As a matter of fact, it was not until some very mysterious attacks started occurring in my life that I began studying and taking witchcraft extremely seriously. Prior to the attacks, I was not doing the topic any justice in my life and ministry. As a matter of fact, I was too empathic towards witches and spent a crazy amount of time praying for their salvation while they were praying for my death. No More! Once I got down to the core of understanding witchcraft, I realized that at least 80% of our spiritual battles are incited by witches and warlocks. And as a result, my new war cry became, SUFFER NOT A WITCH TO LIVE against witches who dare to shoot death arrows of attack in my direction (Exodus 22:18). I am bold about my declarations to send all gifts from the enemy BACK to the sender. This is the way that I choose to war and it works. And if God chooses to intervene with salvation, awesome.

What Is Witchcraft?

I will do my very best to simplify witchcraft so that you will walk away with a basic, but solid, understanding of what it is and some of its operations. Witchcraft is simply the wicked works/craft of witches and warlocks. Witches network with other witches, demons, and fallen angels of all ranks with the purpose of controlling, bending, or swaying a person's life and will in their direction. They do this in an effort to mute out the individual's God-given assignment and destiny. If they had their way, the end result would always lead to death if not stopped.

Witchcraft has many levels of evil, with one being included in the list of acts of the flesh as outlined in Galatians 5:19-21. They use such weapons such as: manipulation, control, intimidation, domination, isolation, soul ties, confusion, sickness, disease, and rejection to trap their victims.

Witches Are Everywhere

It is illegal for demons or fallen angels to freely walk the earth because they are spirits, and need your body in order to do their evil. Human agents—such as witches and warlocks, enter into covenants with the kingdom of darkness, giving them their allegiance to legally decree and declare their evil works in the earth's realm through them. Just like it seems that there are churches on every corner, witches have set up shop on every corner as well. You may know them and their works as: psychics, palm readers, white/black magic, fetish priests, shamans, spiritualists, seers, witch doctors, herbalists, wiccans, obeah, voodoo, santeria, sangomas, and root.

A person who consults a witch is not necessarily a witch but rather, a participant of witchcraft. One of the many dangers that participants of witchcraft face is that is that in the realm of the spirit, they can be labeled, a blind witch and perceive it not. Meaning, witches and warlocks use them to do their dirty work during their sleep state. The involvement in witchcraft initiated them into witchship without their consent. In the realm of the spirit, they are spiritually caged and paralyzed. They are the epitome of the walking dead.

Many times, you cannot identify witches or participants of witchcraft unless the Holy Spirit reveals their identity. And please, do not be naive, witches do not have a signature look but rather, signature works. Modern day witches look just like you and I. Witches or participants of witchcraft could be your spouse, mother, father, cousin, aunt, uncle, grandmother, grandfather, sibling, child, friend, enemy, coworker, neighbor, professor, pastor, church leader, prayer partner, or favorite prophet. As previously stated, you wouldn't know unless God opens your eyes.

In my opinion, the unknown witches are the most dangerous because they are so close and you perceive it not outside of the manifestation of their attacks. Ignorantly, you feed such individuals information regarding your life without discernment. Think about it, has your quality of life diminished or improved since connecting with a certain individual? What leaves your hands after disclosure? What are your dreams showing you? What is your spirit man alerting you to?

Witchcraft Can't Affect Me

I heard the most hideous statement recently, "Witchcraft cannot affect you if you do not believe in it." Let me correct this lie straight from the pit of hell, you do not have to believe in witchcraft for it to affect your life. When witchcraft is in operation, it usually paralyzes the unsuspecting person's ability to discern its works. They become bewitched like prey entangled in a spider's web. The spider of witchcraft lays down its web and stings its prey with just enough venom to paralyze it before devouring it. The prey never saw it coming but experienced the manifestations associated with the trap. I want you to hear me and hear me well; people who do not believe in witchcraft are already bewitched.

The Works of Witchcraft

Beloved, witchcraft is nothing to play with, and must be taken very seriously especially for those of you with a strong call of God on your life. Your life must be surrounded by fire and the blood of Jesus. Forget the ways of the world. You must know that holiness is still right! Reader, these intentional workers of iniquity are absolutely evil. Depending upon their rank, some drink blood and eat flesh paired with a disciplined life of prayer and fasting to their god, Satan. That's how sold out they are to the cause of darkness and infecting as many as possible with the virus of defilement that cancels the glory of God on lives. And this is WHY I pray, "Suffer not a witch nor their works to live."

Witchcraft powers bury destinies, wreck marriages, ruin families, cause sicknesses and disease, accidents, and untimely deaths. They order abortions, miscarriages, and stillbirths. They cause hair loss, weight gain, and programmed evil patterns. These powers mute out the light of God in their unsuspecting target's life and chain them spiritually. They can place demonic marks on a person that orders demonic attacks of rejection, retrogression, shame and dishonor wherever they go. They can attract a person to destiny demoters, and blind a person's spiritual sight. They cause ungodly delay; especially in the area of marriage. They cast love spells and cause seemingly uncontrollable sexual perversion. These powers can cause mental breaks and confusion in the mind; thusly causing a person to question their sanity. They can also cause addictions of all kinds and incite suicide. They love causing financial hardships, and manipulating a person's emotions to the point of making them seem unstable. They shift atmospheres and hinder prayers from ascending to the throne of God. They fight against the fulfillment of prophecies and exchange uncommon destinies for common destinies. Witchcraft unaddressed can reduce a person to absolutely nothing. UGH, suffer NOT a witch to live!

21 Do not I hate them, O Lord, that hate thee? and am not I grieved with those that rise up against thee? 22 I hate them with perfect hatred: I count them mine enemies. Psalm 139:21-22

Weapons Prospering

Just like everything else we have discussed in this book, weapons are allowed to form against you when there is a breech, of some sort, in your foundation. Food for thought, witchcraft is sent to a person by human agents. When you are under attack, someone that you know or someone with an interest in your life or territory that you occupy has sent it. Unfortunately, any random person can give you over by consulting an agent of darkness. If you do not believe it, check eBay or Etsy in order to observe just how easy it is to purchase a curse and send it to someone that you know. However, little do these people know, the trap they set up for another is the very trap that will also ensnare them.

In the middle of writing this book I walked a young woman through deliverance who manifested a witchcraft spirit that was sent to keep her bound. It took close to forty-five minutes to break her free. The spirit communicated that her ex-husband spent thousands of dollars over several years to lock up her destiny. The spirit communicated that her destiny was sealed in a box representing her being bound. It was pleasurable breaking her free in the name of Jesus.

Witchcraft spells are especially eager to work against individuals with the potential to damage their dark kingdom. However, they cannot fulfill their God-given purpose because their lives are filled with sin. Therefore, the works of witchcraft succeed without much resistance. Going into the enemy's camp for answers, or to affect another person's life, is a guarantee that witchcraft will attach itself to a person's life. Some witchcraft problems are actually bloodline issues stemming from witchcraft being practiced. Finally, witchcraft can access a person by being connected to the wrong persons. They are basically guilty by association.

Items of Contact

Workers of certain types of witchcraft use items with your DNA attached to it (e.g. clothing, hair, fingernails, and menstrual pads) in order to curse you in various ways. Those items are called, points of contact. They even use pictures as a point of contact to pray spells over it towards your demise. They can astral project into a person's home and have sex with them, curse them, or manipulate their surroundings. They can even affect and irritate your animals, unsuspecting family members, and friends in order to irritate or attack you. A very common way that they make contact is through food. Ensure that you say grace over your food consistently, and try your best not to allow your stomach to lead you. Do not eat from random people and places.

Forego Witchcraft Practices

As Christians, you SHOULD NOT burn sage, mop with turpentine, wear garlic, wipe down walls with ammonia, nor throw salt around your house in an effort to ward off evil spirits. Those are practices that are used in witchcraft to drive off evil spirits and when you do such, you are ignorantly operating in witchcraft. Leave those types of practices for those who have no hope! Christians drive spirits out in the name of Jesus and by the blood! Just think, if sage can ward off evil, eat it and you should be instantly delivered!

Children & Witchcraft

One of the easiest and most common ways that a child can become initiated into witchcraft is through the celebration of the most demonic holiday on the face of the earth; Halloween. Without researching the origin of Halloween (and other pagan based holidays), eager parents dress their children up in demonic characters and Greek gods aka, super heroes. They then take their children from door to door begging for candy from people that they do not know. These innocent babies unknowingly become targets of the enemy's devices by associating with a day that they should be shielded from.

Instead of rolling your eyes and sighing, remember, the enemy does not play fair! All he needs are legal rights. Such ignorance is excusable for the world but definitely not Christians! Without knowing a single thing about the origins of Halloween, spiritual discernment should kick in warning that light and darkness have no business communing together. How is God glorified in blood, skeletons, jack o' lanterns, spiders, death, witches, spells, ghosts, goblins and vampires?

Would you take Jesus trick or treating? And if so, what would be his costume? If you believe that my question is silly and irrelevant, reflect on why I would ask such a question. The spirit of God resides within us and instead of teaching our children spiritual discipline and fleshly denial, many of our churches hold alternative festivals in an attempt to appease you and your children. Some of the churches of this day and age remind me of the children of Israel whom time and time again forfeited their peculiarity because they wandered after the ways of the world. We have been instructed to come from out of her for a reason! The world is corrupt because she loves the darkness and we are clearly instructed to be the complete opposite; light.

Churches who profess Christ as their savior should steer clear of Halloween and teach their youth the truth. Did you know that witches distribute candy that they have prayed time-released curses over that will not only affect your children, but also your home in the most bizarre ways? Furthermore, Halloween is a big day for Satanists, occultists and witches. They often perform rituals, hold wild parties, offer blood sacrifices to their god(s), perform sexual orgies and child molestation, contact the dead, and release curses in the land in observance of their holiday.

I recall while working for the State of Alabama as a social worker, I was sent to investigate a report of child neglect at one of the local high schools on Halloween. When I arrived at the school, I was informed that the child was absent. I went to the home in order to show a second attempt at contact. To my surprise, the student answered the door. He was there with a friend. They informed me that they were Wiccan and stayed home in order to celebrate Halloween because it was considered a holiday for them. Utilizing my badge, I informed him that I needed to investigate further. I was invited into the home where candles were lit and strange music was playing. I was not moved because I knew that the blood of Jesus was covering me. Nevertheless, I did not waste time hanging around. As soon as I exited the home, I went into prayer. That was my very first up close and personal introduction to witches and their craft. While Christian parents are picking up costumes and candy, dark and sinister forces are laying traps for the ignorant or simply rebellious Christians. Reader, do your homework! My break down does this topic no serious justice whatsoever.

Dumb Sheep

Our spirit man is very sensitive to witchcraft, but most have been programmed through religion to downplay their ability to hear from God independently. Unfortunately, far too many religious institutions operate under strong powers of witchcraft. They use their manipulating and controlling powers to raise dumb sheep. Reader, there is a difference in intelligently submitting versus dumbly sitting. These poor babies must run everything, just as I did, by a perceived higher-ranking Christian.

This is now laughable to me because spiritual dependency contradicts what Jesus did on the cross. We were reconciled back unto God when he died for us. The veil was ripped from top to bottom. We are under a new covenant and can now go directly to God in order to commune with him (see Hebrew 4:16, Hebrews 9:8-9, Hebrews 10:19-20). Because of the finished work of the cross, we no longer need a middle man or sacrifices. He is eager to commune with and instruct His babies (see Hebrews 4:14-16).

I am not saying that seeking Godly counsel is bad. As a matter of fact, the Bible instructs us that safety is found in the multitude of counsel (see Proverbs 15:22). I personally believe that Godly counsel esteems you and fosters your maturity in Christ. Godly counsel is beneficial in fine tuning your spiritual ears while mature Christians are offered the opportunity to present their opinion on your matter. Such people are quick to dismiss their ability to hear God and trust what they discern.

I overcame the powers of church witchcraft by making up in my mind that I would make my own spiritual decisions and trust my ability to hear. Therefore, I would have to take full responsibility for getting it right or wrong before God. I cannot begin to describe the freedom that accompanies my decision. I have a God versus man dependency. Be advised that no one should be speaking into your ear louder than God. Do not allow anyone to feed you the word without studying for yourself.

Just know that you will fight plenty of witchcraft battles even after deliverance, and there is absolutely nothing that you can do about it. They are simply sold out for their cause and doing their job. Sell out for your cause and do yours. There is no need for you to fear the works of the enemy, because you will be more than equipped to send the enemy packing once you connect with this ministry and hang around long enough.

The word of God informs us that weapons will form but they will not prosper. You should know by now that you must utilize your God-given authority in order for those weapons not to prosper. Go ahead and ask your pressing question, "Minister Faithe do you truly pray, 'Suffer not a witch to live?'" Ha! *You Already Know!*

Soul Work:

Do you see the workings of witchcraft in your life? If yes, in what areas?

How has witchcraft affected your life?

Prayer:

Father, I acknowledge that I am being controlled by witchcraft. I submit my mind, will, and thoughts to you in the name of Jesus.

Prayer Point:

Witchcraft, no longer will I be controlled or manipulated by the wicked influence attempting to operate in my life.

Chapter Terms:

Witchcraft: a network of witches (female), warlocks (male), demons, wizards, and fallen angels of many ranks that work together using sorcery in order to control, bend, or sway a person's will in their direction. Warlock: a man who practices witchcraft; a sorcerer. Witch: a female who practices witchcraft

(see Appendix C for witchcraft breaking prayer)

Dreams Really Do Come True

Chapter 13

I have found that the contents of a person's dreams are a major giveaway regarding the who, what, and whys of demonic oppression. Your dreams show you what weapons are forming for and against you in the spirit realm. People normally do not have face-to-face encounters with demons. Demons usually present themselves to a person in dreams; more so, than in the natural. Dreams are important and I would be doing you a huge disservice if I did not address the topic. You need to know as much as possible about dreams because they really do come true.

Many people have reported seeing demons in their dreams and/or sensing their presence around them. I would dare to speculate that most people have had direct and symbolic encounters with demons in their dreams, but did not know it because of a lack of knowledge. Possessing an inability to interpret the symbols, they failed to address the dream spiritually and disregarded it with a chuckle or shrug of the shoulder. When I began my journey, one of the first things God did was teach me how to understand and interpret dreams.

He did this by placing the desire for understanding within me, and the hunt led me to the discovery of legitimate resources. What I learned stunned me. The enemy had been showing himself to me in my dreams for quite some time and I understood it not. For me, the dream root extended back to my childhood. The thought of how different things would have been had I understood my dreams fuels my passion for helping you understand yours. I thank God for what I now know and for the ability to apply it. Honestly, I have been saved from a lot of hurt and pain because I now understand my dreams. I have also experienced a lot of success because of this skill. The enemy can no longer show up in my dreams and think that I am going to just bow down and accept his prophecies. Dreams really do come true, and there is no way that he can freely have a say in my truth anymore unless I become spiritually lazy. Those days are long gone and soon, you too, will be able to say the same.

Let me be very clear, I am not an expert on dreams. Since this is not a book on dreams, I will not attempt to share with you even a fraction of the knowledge I have accumulated over the years regarding dreams. I will, however, focus on addressing dreams as they pertain to demonic oppression.

The Purpose of Dreams

It is tragic that so many people dismiss their dreams. The purpose of dreams is to show you what spiritual weapons are operating for or against you in the spirit realm. Dreams can give you a glance of the state of your soul and a peek into your future. Dreams also give physical form to what you cannot see in the natural. For instance, you cannot see the demon that is affecting your life in the natural but he may reveal himself to you in a dream. Dreams can indicate whether or not you are on course spiritually, financially, and educationally. Dreams are a blessing because they educate, comfort, warn, and instruct. They give you insight regarding the Father and enemy's heart concerning you. Dreams can be symbolic or direct. Unlike symbolic dreams, direct dreams require very little interpretation. It is important to invest time in learning the various symbols associated with dreams. For example, dreaming about your father in a dream may symbolize, God the father or your earthly father. In order to determine which, you must analyze the context of the dream. Once you learn the most common symbols, you will be in an amazing position to interpret your dreams with great accuracy. Job 33:14-18 states:

For God does speak-now one way, now another-though no one perceives it. In a dream, in a vision of the night, when deep sleep falls on people as they slumber in their beds, he may speak in their ears and terrify them with warnings, to turn them from wrong doing and keep them from pride, to preserve them from the pit, their lives from perishing by the sword (NIV).

What's the Big Deal?

Let us be honest, we are in a spiritual battle that spills over into the natural realm. Matthew 13:24-30 explains this by stating:

Jesus told them another parable: *"The kingdom of heaven is like a man who sowed good seed in his field. But while everyone was sleeping, his enemy came and sowed weeds among the wheat, and went away. When the wheat sprouted and formed heads, then the weeds also appeared. The owner's servants came to him and said, 'Sir, didn't you sow good seed in your field? Where then did the weeds come from?' 'An enemy did this,' he replied. The servants asked him, 'Do you want us to go and pull them up?' 'No,' he answered, 'because while you are pulling the weeds, you may uproot the wheat with them. Let both grow together until the harvest. At that time I will tell the harvesters: First, collect the weeds and tie them in bundles to be burned; then gather the wheat and bring it into my barn"* (NIV).

The enemy operates in the dark, and trust me, you do not want any part of the crop he plants. He sows discord while we are in our most vulnerable state, sleep. Keep in mind that we are spirits housed in a shell called the body. The spirit realm is not governed by time, so you possess the ability to see what God and the devil are planning for you before it ever manifests. I can promise you that every major occurrence in your life, whether good or bad, was ordered in the spirit realm first.

Opened Eyes

When you dream, you are seeing into a realm from which your spirit man originated. It is the realm where God and Satan reside. According to 2 Corinthians 12:2, God resides in the third heaven and Satan resides in the second. If God opened your eyes, you would likely die of a heart attack because you would be overwhelmed by what you saw. You would see demonic and angelic activity all around you. You would behold grotesque creatures and battles taking place around you. You would be able to see just how much Satan interferes in your everyday affairs. As a result, your tune would change regarding giving him too much credit, and you would certainly acknowledge that we do not give him enough credit. Even so, please allow me to pause and give thanks to all of the angels of God who refused Satan. Thank you for serving humanity (Hebrews 1:14). You are very well appreciated.

There are times that God will open a person's spiritual eyes and allow him or her to see His angels. However, it is almost always for ministry purposes when God allows you to see demons. When people talk about high ranking secret societies–such as the Illuminati, or the third eye–they are actually talking about seeing into the spirit realm and conversing with various ranks of fallen angels in pursuit of a higher level of knowledge. Once people give themselves over to Satan, seeing and operating on the demonic side of the spirit realm becomes their norm. The things they do would absolutely blow your mind. They understand that tapping into this realm takes them to levels we cannot fathom. Perhaps you know exactly what I am referring to because you used to be or you are still a part of that world. This information may sound exciting but I can assure you that exploring that realm through Satan will seal your fate in hell. We, as Christians, are forbidden to tap into such because it is offensive to God.

Explore the following texts:

- Exodus 22:18 • Leviticus 19:31 • Leviticus 20:6, 27 • Deuteronomy 18:9-12 • 1 Samuel 15:23 • 2 Kings 21:6 • 1 Chronicles 10:13-14 • 2 Chronicles 33:6 • Isaiah 8:19 • Isaiah 19:3 • Acts 19:19 • Galatians 5:19-21 • Revelation 21:8 • Revelation 22:15

Types of Dreams

1. Demonic dreams. People who suffer from horrific nightmares experience terror that paralyzes them with fear. These dreams come from the demonic world and are meant to sow fear in the lives of their victims. Even so, not all demonic dreams bring terror. There are demons that show up in a very seducing and cunning manner. When a person begins to speak the language of the spirit realm, the demons assigned to their lives will begin to expose themselves and the legal right associated with their oppression.
2. Soul dreams. There are dreams that come from your soul. Soul dreams usually express events or emotions that you formerly or are currently experiencing in life. Soul dreams often pinpoint unhealed areas of your life and expose what you don't desire to face. They highlight soul ties, offenses, unforgiveness, and secret desires.
3. Spirit man. Spirit dreams usually point out character flaws and areas that the Holy Spirit would like to correct and mature in your life. Spirit man dreams also expose the state of your heart thusly propelling you into repentance.
4. Spirit of God. These dreams come straight from God. They usually involve warnings, instructions, or insight pertaining to your life and the lives of others.

Who Dreams?

Everyone dreams and fall into one of three distinct categories.

1. Those who do not dream. These individuals believe that they do not dream, but they do. They are dreaming but have great difficulty remembering their dreams. The enemy can block a person's ability to recall their dreams. In most cases, this is an indication of spiritual contamination, poor bedtime habits, interference due to heavy medication and/or a very weak spiritual state. The enemy or poor habits slam the door of their awareness shut tight.
2. Those with scattered dream recollection. These individuals dream but the dream snatcher erases their memory before they can recall their dreams. They awake with a foggy recollection of what they dreamt. The pieces are scattered. They have no way of combating or protecting what was shown to them. More than likely, demonic weapons form and prosper against them, that otherwise would have been cancelled. Prophecies are blocked that otherwise would have been protected. Many factors can contribute to this, but it is usually because their spirit man is not as strong as it needs to be.
3. Those with dream recollection. This is the best position to be in. The ability to recall your dreams is stellar. Especially the ones that show a need for intervention or protection. These individuals are blessed to be able to recall their dreams. However, unfortunately, in most cases, they are not able to interpret, refute, or protect them.

What Should I Do About My Dreams?

I stopped interpreting dreams for random people long ago because it is very time consuming, and because the power is not only in understanding your dreams but in what you do with the understanding.

I observed that most people who reached out to me for dream interpretation were not willing to put in the work to protect or cancel the dream. They just wanted the interpretation. They failed to understand that dreams really do come true and it takes a response to stop and block what isn't godly. It also takes action to protect what is. When you have a bad dream, you must cancel it immediately upon waking up. Depending upon the strength of the dream, it must be met with violent spiritual warfare prayers and fasting. If the dream was good, pray God's protection over it so that the enemy cannot uproot it.

How Often Should I Dream?

There is no set number regarding dreams but I will give you an idea which one of the three categories you fall into. Keep in mind that it's not the quantity but quality of your dreams that matters. The goal is for your godly dreams to outweigh your demonic dreams. This will happen as you dismantle the works of darkness and seek the heart of God above all else.

1. High volume: 12 or more meaningful dreams per month.
2. Medium volume: 7 to 9 meaningful dreams per month.
3. Low volume: 1 to 4 meaningful dreams per month.

Common Dreams and Their Symbols

I have compiled a list of common dreams relating to spiritual warfare. When trying to interpret a dream, you must be sure to pay close attention to colors, numbers, smells, and your mood. Dreams from God are usually filled with color and emotions that do not leave you feeling scared, depressed, and anxious. The enemy's dreams are the polar opposite and leave you feeling like something just is not right.

1. **Sex:** Having sex in your dreams with a known or unknown person is an indication of demonic defilement. It is also an

indication that you have a spirit spouse. Maintaining a stable relationship and breaking into your marital destiny may prove very difficult.

2. **Getting married:** Depending upon the context, seeing yourself getting married to an unknown or known person or is an indication that you have a spirit spouse. The marriage indicates that you have entered into covenant with it. Maintaining a stable relationship and breaking into your marital destiny may prove very difficult.

3. **Snakes:** Represent witchcraft spirits that have been sent to attack your life. The type of snake also makes a difference and can give insight regarding their assignment. Snakes can also represent an undercover enemy (frenemy) in your midst. A group of snakes can represent organizational enemies.

4. **Coffin:** Seeing a coffin or yourself in a coffin indicates that the spirit of death is hunting you.

5. Sitting for an exam repeatedly: This is a sign that your life is programmed with cycler hardship and struggle.

6. **Reoccurring dreams:** You are stuck on the same life level for an extended period of time, and you cannot progress. This type of dream is also an indication that a particular matter has not been resolved and demands your attention.

7. Stolen, missing, or spotted wedding dress: There is a demonic attack against your marital destiny.

8. **Blocked doors:** You are being denied open doors of opportunity.

9. **Kissing or Being Kissed:** Betrayal is lurking in your life. Depending upon the context of the dream, it can also mean, covenant or a presence of lust.

10. **Reoccurring dreams of past events and/or places:** There are spirits assigned to keep you locked in the past, and to prevent your moving forward. These dreams can also represent the

origin of unresolved emotional issues and/or demonic strongholds.

11. **Dead relatives:** These are familiar spirits of deception that have been sent to monitor you. Seeing the same dead relative can represent a demonic soul tie or the transfer and reinforcement of a family curse.
12. **Strange creatures fighting you**: This is an indication of demonic oppression in your life, primarily from the forest kingdom.
13. **You see yourself rising and suddenly falling:** This is a sign of demonic setbacks sent to prevent you from advancing in life. You get very close to achievement, and then you are knocked down.
14. **Stolen shoes:** Your ability to successfully do God's work is being blocked. It can also represent disgrace, shame and/or poverty.
15. **Stuck in traffic:** The enemy is delaying your arrival to your destination.
16. Seeing yourself naked: The enemy is insisting upon bringing shame into your life or he is using your hidden shame against you.
17. **Slow-moving creatures:** These types of dream symbolizes that a spirit of slow progress is operating in your life. No matter how hard you try, things are moving for you at a very slow pace (e.g. snails, slug, turtles and sloths).
18. **Chained or imprisoned:** You are in spiritual bondage and a slave to the enemy in the spirit realm.
19. **Repetitive dreams of an old place of employment:** The enemy is blocking your promotion by keeping you on an old level, or you have an old workplace soul wound that needs to be addressed.

20. **Always arriving late**: Lateness is indication of missed opportunities or remaining steps behind because of demonic distractions or blockages.
21. **Rats and roaches:** Such dreams indicate that unclean spirits of defilement are dwelling in your home or body.
22. Stolen seat: This dream indicates the inability to settle down into your resting place in life due to demonic activity.
23. **Crying:** Depending upon the context, an indication of impending sorrow or sadness in your life.
24. **Sexual orgies, porn, homosexual acts, or exposure of sex organs:** The spirit of lust and perversion is operating in your life or trying to gain entry. It can also mean that one or some of your associates carry the spirit of lust and/or perversion.
25. **Losing blood:** Your life virtues are being drained by demonic entities.
26. **Dreaming of old lover(s):** Old lover dreams can indicate an unresolved soul tie, unresolved offense, or an indication that the person(s) will resurface in your life soon.
27. **Driven by an unknown person to an unknown destination:** You are not in control of your destiny. You are either being driven to an evil destination or being influenced by the driver.
28. **Roaming aimlessly:** You lack vision and purpose, and are possibly under a witchcraft spell against your ability to settle down in life.
29. **Someone cutting or shaving off your hair**: Your glory is under attack or being stolen.
30. **Someone straightening your hair**: The enemy is attempting to make your glory common and void of uniqueness.
31. **Being shot at or chased:** Those are signs of demons on assignment to destroy your life.
32. **Ants, rats, roaches, tattered clothing, losing property, finding coins, spending money, or losing your purse or wallet:** These

are signs of poverty at work in your life and/or that you will suffer a loss to your property.
33. **Losing or damaging your phone:** Your connection with God is lost, weak, or under attack.
34. **Losing teeth:** You are losing foundational spiritual truths or a loss of wisdom.
35. **Drunkenness/alcoholism:** A spirit of alcohol addiction has been sent into your life.
36. **Hit on the head:** A spirit of confusion or mental illness has been sent your way.
37. **Spider webs:** Demonic entanglement and traps, such as a web of confusion and lies, are being planned against you.
38. Spiders: Spiders represent an alter of rejection and hate has been sent into your life.
39. **Often swimming or bathing in large bodies of water:** You are connected to the marine kingdom. The marine kingdom is a spiritual city under various bodies of water. Their number one assignment is sexual perversion.
40. **Fighting with family or friends**: Those specific relationships are under demonic attack. Arrows of confusion and strife have been sent to destroy the relationship. This type of dream can also indicate an unaddressed soul wound.
41. **Ants:** Serving and working hard and faithfully without pay or profit.
42. **Dogs:** Depending upon the context of the dream, a strong witchcraft spirit of lust, a monitoring spirit, or a spirit of intimidation designed to prevent advancement and to scatter you.
43. **Cats:** Cats can represent family spirits or betrayal. They can also represent household wickedness.
44. **Shopping but not locating your size:** The enemy is denying you the desires of your heart that you have worked and prayed

for. It also indicates that a spirit of denied access is operating in your life.
45. **Animals chasing you:** You are close to a breakthrough but ancestral demons are trying to stop it. Such dreams may also represent entities attempting to scatter you.
46. **Constantly running:** The enemy is sending many situations designed to keep you busy, on the defense and ultimately prevent you from resting.
47. **Missing a flight:** You have been programmed to miss an important opportunity.
48. **Missing keys:** Your access to open doors has been stolen. The enemy is after your authority.
49. **Police:** Bloodline witches have been sent to harass, delay and/or arrest you in the spirit realm.
50. **Seeing items disappear from your life:** The enemy has stolen something from you that God has released. Pay very close attention to what is stolen.
51. **Eating:** The act can indicate witchcraft initiation and/or being fed sickness and disease. The purpose is to strengthen ancestral covenants and/or weaken you spiritually.
52. **Blocked by a large body of water:** You are experiencing blockage, delay, and opposition from the marine kingdom.
53. **People laughing at and mocking you**: These dreams represent gossip and the slandering of your name, jealousy, or evil plots against you. It also represents evil alters of rejection.
54. **Broken items or damage to property:** A plot to attack your possessions is being devised. This is a delay device.
55. **Robbery:** The enemy is planning to AGGRESSIVELY take something from you.
56. **Frogs:** Frogs represent unclean spirits that affect several areas of your life. They jump from area to area.
57. **Alarm clock going off**: This is a Warning or indication that you are running out of time.

58. **Music played that seduces you:** Hoodoo has been sent to bewitch you in order to carry out evil intent.
59. **Talking to strange people and traveling to strange places:** This is an indication that you have been initiated into witchcraft without your consent.
60. **Accidents:** You are being warned of impending danger.
61. **Miscarriage:** The enemy has ordered plans to abort your pregnancy or what you are birthing in the spirit realm.
62. **Being hit in your pregnant belly:** The enemy has sent a death sentence to your fetus.
63. **Giving birth to or suckling an unknown child that you believe to be yours:** This is an indication that you have a child, or children, in the marine kingdom with the spirit husband.

Soul Work:

What is your dream world like?

Are you concerned by your answer? If yes, why?

Prayer:

Heavenly Father, please help me learn how to interpret my dreams.

Prayer Point:

I command all demonic agents disturbing me while I sleep to drown in the blood of Jesus.

(see Appendix D for dream symbols prayer points)

The Race to the Right House

Chapter 14

If you are easily offended, I encourage you to skip this chapter because the enemy would love to block your deliverance by offending you. By now you should have picked up on the fact that I am very bold and honest! In this chapter, I speak very candidly about racism in America. I believe whole-heartedly that change cannot come without first addressing the root cause and embracing honesty for the sake of winning the race to the Right House.

The 2016 presidential election was one of the most exciting elections in American history, aside from the election of America's first black President–mild-mannered and charming Barack Obama. Regardless of your personal opinion, Barack Obama represented the United States well throughout his professional career. He was a scandal-free lawyer, former Chicago Senator, Harvard graduate, and the 44th president of the United State. His beautiful wife, Michelle Obama, is a wholesome lawyer, Princeton and Harvard graduate, and health advocate.

The Obamas and their children handled the presidency with dignity and grace. First Lady Obama was insulted by Pamela Ramsey Taylor, the director of a non-profit government organization in West Virginia. Ms. Taylor posted that she was tired of seeing an "ape in heels" and that it will be "refreshing" to finally have "a classy, beautiful, and dignified" First Lady. Taylor was not the first influential person to make similar racist remarks or insinuations. Taylor was later joined by Beverly Whaling, mayor of Clay, West Virginia; Dan Johnson, a Kentucky state legislative candidate; Charles Wasko, mayor of West York Pennsylvania; Patrick Rushing, mayor of Airway Heights,

Washington; and Rusty DePass, former chairman of the state election commission in South Carolina.

Notable political scholars agree that President Obama received more opposition than any other president in recent American history. Although many would argue that it was because of his policies, any conscious observer and truth-bearer would admit it was primarily because of the color of his skin. Too many Americans were not ready for nor welcoming of a negro president. Every decision and move he made was magnified and scrutinized beyond the norm as a result of this. He and his family were called niggers, apes, primates, and gorillas. Conservatives desperately tried to paint Mrs. Obama as an angry black woman. When that tactic did not work, they attacked her attire and attempted to diminish her intelligence and class. President Obama was often depicted as a monkey with large ears. He was also repeatedly accused of being a Muslim and not an American citizen.

Forced to play the political game, President Obama was forced to renounce his pastor, Jeremiah Wright over divisive comments he made regarding racism in America. Conservatives retorted that a president connected to such an individual must share the same views. As if it was a crime, groves of angry white Americans lashed out at dark-skinned people for voting President Obama into office while celebrating his blackness. To their utter disgust, President Obama served two terms in the White House and gave America his best.

The 2016 election introduced to the stage a crass candidate by the name of Donald Trump. The billionaire reality TV star holds a bachelor's degree and absolutely no political experience. He came on the scene with the notion that it was his duty to make America great again. A man who showed no fruit of the Spirit suddenly became God's chosen vessel; at least that is how millions of Evangelicals tell it. No matter how many people and cultures he insulted and how much hate he incited, Trump was heralded as a hero by millions of angry, predominately white Americans who felt forgotten or oppressed under President Obama's presidency and blackness.

To make matters worse, the moral fiber in which the United States Presidency had been established on became tarnished by Trump. Accusations of sexual misconduct against a lawsuit-plagued, tax-evading, casino building, non-military serving, and inexperienced politician on marriage number three meant absolutely nothing to many American citizens. In fact, a video surfaced showing the non-religious presidential candidate making disgusting comments that glorified adultery and demeaning women. Sadly to say, it was brushed aside as being "locker room talk." Trump's nasty tactics during his campaigns included inviting President Obama's Republican half-brother to the third presidential debate, encouraging his supporters to exhibit violence toward those who opposed him, and inviting women who accused former President Bill Clinton of sexual harassment to one of his debates against his opponent, the wife of former President, Bill Clinton.

Ironically, Trump is married to a beautiful immigrant, Melania Trump; a woman with a slew of racy, nude photos all over the internet. Mrs. Trump blatantly plagiarized parts of one of Former First Lady Michelle Obama's speeches to the Republican National Convention. In spite of the facts, his insistence that he would "Make America Great Again" catapulted Mr. Trump into the highest office in the land, and the less-than-wholesome Melania Trump was suddenly deemed First Lady material. Mr. Trump landed a victory and his supporters called it God's sovereign will when in fact, it was America's sick sovereign will. One of Trump's first moves was to appoint a white nationalist, Stephen Bannon, as his campaign manager and as his chief White House strategist. Bannon has been justly accused of making anti-Semitic comments in the past. Not once did his born-again supporters request that he distance himself from such a divisive individual. So, I am guessing that you are probably asking how is all of this important, and what does it have to do with deliverance? I will provide you with a valid explanation. Keep reading.

America's Sickness

I chose to highlight Barack Obama and Donald Trump because this is an excellent example of America's hypocrisy. I contrasted these two families in an attempt to illuminate just how imbalanced the equality scale truly is. When one takes an unbiased step back and weighs the dynamics of both candidates, the facts are startling and clearly highlight America's untreated sickness of racism. Trump brilliantly took a page from Richard Nixon's playbook, Southern Strategy, and played on the sickness of America in order to make his way into the White House. I will not say, for a single moment, that Hillary Clinton was the best choice for America any more than I will say that Donald Trump is the worst choice for America. However, I will say that the 2016 election highlighted just how divided America is, and how desperately she needs healing and deliverance.

I often say that deliverance must take place on a micro, meso, and macro level. As it is, America is too divided to say that she is a nation after God's heart. Specifically, the church in America is even more divided and racism exists on both sides of the divide. I am especially saddened and grieved by the many Caucasian men and women of the gospel who aggressively campaigned for such a divisive candidate, but remained silent on issues and celebrations that affect brown and yellow people. I am disheartened by white, brown, and yellow men and women of the gospel who adopted a position of silence rather than taking a stand for justice and liberty for all. Shame on them! I do not believe for one minute that this past election was about righteousness.

If it were, Republicans and Democrats would walk it out in their everyday lives no matter who's in office.

John 13:35 reminds us that people will know we are Jesus' disciples by our love for one another. Spiritual abuse and misuse of God-granted platforms is a dangerous game. It is never okay to mistreat your neighbor because they do not believe as you do. By no means am I saying we should not promote righteousness and be empathetic to sin instead. I am simply saying that you cannot promote righteousness while demoting the heart issues of another person and say it is of God. As a Christian, what affects your brothers and sisters in Christ should affect you also. Why is it okay to pray for a president who looks like you but not for one who does not? Why does God have so much to say about one political party over the other? It is simple, He does not. Let me suggest that God is neither Republican nor Democrat, He is Kingdom. Wake up, Zion! Abortion and same-sex marriages are symptoms of a much deeper problem. The enemy is so crafty that he has us fighting each other instead of him.

Case in point, ignorance at its best would be the notion that all Democrats do not believe in God, and are applauders of abortion and same-sex marriages. Could it be that people sway to the side that gives them the right to choose rather than the side that wants their vote without soul contact? Only a closed-minded person would truly believe that all Republicans are Christians, uneducated, and racist. Could it be that it is not what one party stands for but what it does not stand for that is the deciding factor? Why are we fighting each other when the Bible makes it crystal clear who our true enemy is? Ephesians 6:12 tells us: "For we wrestle not against flesh and blood, but against principalities, against powers, against the rulers of the darkness of this world, against spiritual wickedness in high places."

The Truth

Considering the weight of legal rights, racism will always be a divide in America because she has blood on her hands. America is a country that was built on stolen land and on the backs of slaves, and she has a long track record of mistreating immigrants. When I compare her to the heart of God, I have to come to the final conclusion that America has never and will never be great unless she repents. It is no different on a micro level than it is on a macro level. If there is a legal right, the enemy will attack and be justified in doing so. America was stinking long before prayer was taken out of schools, abortion was legalized, and gay marriage was embraced. As long as we look at each other and see color and differences, God cannot receive the glory He rightfully deserves.

Just as Trump took a play from Nixon's playbook, Satan took one from God's. God used the incident at the Tower of Babel to divide the people's tongues to keep them from uniting against His perfect will. Similarly, Satan, the master counterfeiter, has created his own plan of division in hopes of keeping the church from uniting; it is called racism. He has implemented a master plan to divide the men and women of God by the color of their skin. Wouldn't you agree that His plan is prospering?

We have all been affected by this sickness in one way or another. We have all said, thought, and/or committed racist atrocities that totally contradict God's heart. Regarding racism, there is too much unforgiveness, bitterness and resentment in the land on all sides, and it is sickening. Sadly, the sickness has a stronghold on the Christian church. The late Reverend Martin Luther King, Jr. stated that "the most segregated hour" in this nation is at 11 o'clock on a Sunday morning. No wonder the world sees the church as a joke! I want you to think about how much damage we could do if we were united. Reader, it is all of our responsibility to examine our hearts and do our duty to destroy the legal rights regarding racism. We must wash the blood on America's hands with the blood of Jesus. We cannot say we are His disciples if we harbor hatred and prejudices against each other. It is noble to desire greatness in the land in which we reside, but let us never forget that this land is not our home. While others are fighting for the White House, let us make a run for the Right House. In the meantime, let us pray that our President will be used to lead this country into repentance. I can hear some of you mumbling, "Minister Faithe, do you truly believe God can use someone like Trump?" My response is, you already know!

Soul Work:

Do you have any hate in your heart towards anyone because of the color of their skin? Why?

If yes, what do you think you can do to fix this?

Prayer:

Heavenly Father, I acknowledge that I have hate in my heart towards (insert race) people. Please teach me how to love people of all races just as you love them.

Prayer Point:

In the name of Jesus, I command any hate towards others to be exposed and eradicated from my life through the blood of Jesus!

What About the Children?

Chapter 14

I always encourage people to teach their children everything they learn about spiritual warfare. The response is always surprising because, interestingly enough, they feel comfortable discussing angels but uncomfortable discussing demons. I lovingly remind them that the enemy attacked them at an early age and their children are not the exception. The enemy does not look at your children and delay his attacks because they are innocent and incapable of protecting themselves. I also remind them that at an early age they were experiencing nightmares, seeing spirits, and hearing voices. I further encourage them to consider that the same bloodline curses affecting their lives are claiming their children too. And what they don't deal with, their children and their children will be forced to contend with.

The truth about demons is not to be feared and hidden; it is to be exposed. It's valuable information. What remains in the dark cannot be confronted or eradicated. Beloved, if your children can watch a horror movie and even celebrate Halloween, surely they are ready and completely capable of understanding the operation of demons in their lives and in the lives of others. If they can sit down and learn how to play a complicated video game, surely they can understand the works of the enemy. How many times have you uttered while reading this book, "Wow! I wish someone had taught me this information at an early age!" Well, let that not be the whispers of your children ten or twenty years from now when they stumble across this book.

My Seed

I am very proud of my son Tyler, who will be eleven soon. He is obedient, an excellent student, an athlete, and has a heart for God. Tyler is very well versed in spiritual warfare, and I love it. My son can define for you what demons are, what a legal right is, and how the enemy enters and manipulates a person's life. He also understands how the enemy pressures us to sin. Without skipping a beat, he can tell you what the bloodline weaknesses are in my family and in his father's family. He knows what he needs to be aware of as he moves forward in life. My son monitors his dreams and knows how to interpret them fairly accurately.

He knows these things, not because I am his mother, but because I took the time to teach him. I refuse to allow the enemy to educate my son. That is my job. I do not expect perfection from him, but I do expect him to honor God until the day he is called home. My son is prepared to die for Christ even now because he knows that it may be a requirement; considering how this world is going. He is prepared mentally because he knows there is life on the other side. I share my struggles with my son in an age-appropriate manner. I bring him in on my prayers so he can experience firsthand what surrender and faith produces. My son will be able to reflect on our spiritual victories as a student, athlete, husband, father, and Christian when challenged by life. He understands the power of God and his God-given authority.

My son came through for me many nights while I was pressing through some pretty hard places. He laid hands on me and beat back the winds of the enemy with the blood of Jesus. I will never forget those moments, and I will always treasure them. It was Tyler who told the enemy that he would not disgrace our family. It was Tyler who told delay to be delayed. It was Tyler who told the enemy to die by fire. You better believe that he will have no problem covering his wife, because he first covered his mother as part of his training.

Take Those Babies Seriously

Parents, take your children seriously when they tell you they are afraid or that they are seeing and/or hearing things. Do not brush them off as just attention seeking. They have no reason to lie to you. Pray with them at night, and anoint their rooms with the blood of Jesus. Read the word of God over them before bed. Teach them how to call on Jesus, not only when they are under attack, but in their everyday affairs as well. Teach them not to be afraid of the enemy. Utilize the prayers in this book, and let them repeat them with you. Pray with them before they leave the house in the mornings, and teach them what honoring God looks like. Train them for war now before it is too late.

It is easier to combat the works of the enemy than to break his hold. Prophesy over their lives by speaking what you desire to see manifest in their lives. If they are exhibiting negative characteristics, speak what you desire to see manifest no matter what. Do not repeat or agree with the enemy's opinion of your children. You are saving your bloodline when training your children to be spiritually conscious. Spiritual awareness and the tools to defend themselves from the kingdom of darkness is the greatest gift you can ever give the fruit of your womb. This pleases God and falls in line with Deuteronomy 11:19-23:

Teach them to your children, talking about them when you sit at home and when you walk along the road, when you lie down and when you get up. Write them on the door frames of your houses and on your gates, so that your days and the days of your children may be many in the land the Lord swore to give your ancestors, as many as the days that the heavens are above the earth. If you carefully observe all these commands I am giving you to follow—to love the Lord your God, to walk in obedience to him and to hold fast to him—then the Lord will drive out all these nations before you, and you will dispossess nations larger and stronger than you (NIV).

I can sense your excitement and the expansion of your vision. You are excited about knowing just how much more you can influence your children. I want you to think about all the ways you were failed as a child. Please do not repeat the cycle with your children. Make a decision right now to change the way you parent when it comes to spiritual things. Instead of making empty noise because prayer was taken out of schools, you need to make sure that there is consistent prayer in your home. If prayer is in your home, it can never be removed from school. God entrusted you with such beautiful babies. Are you seriously going to allow the enemy to raise them? Are you going to continue taking a passive role in their lives? I hope not! You do not mind telling off anyone else who crosses you concerning them, so why would you continue giving the enemy a free pass? You should not! Now is the time for you to stand up and tell the enemy to back off concerning your seed. What happens when a mother and father stand up and defend their offspring in the spirit? You already know!

Soul Work:

If you have children, can you honestly say that you have been investing in them spiritually? 2. Moving forward, if anything, what will you do differently?

Prayer:

Father, I dedicate my child(ren) to you for your glory. Please help me to be the kind of parent that heaven will agree with.

Prayer Point:

I decree and declare that all of the days of my child(ren) are blessed.

This Thing Called Deliverance

Chapter 16

People usually have a slew of questions when they contact me for deliverance and rightfully so. If everything you know about deliverance came from horror movies or overly zealous evangelicals, deliverance can seem extremely intimidating or downright scary. In this chapter, I will attempt to address some of the most common questions I've received regarding deliverance.

What is deliverance?

In this particular context, deliverance is the act of enforcing the authority of God as dictated in Luke 10:19, to cast demons out of a person's body. Some may refer to it as an exorcism. I do not use that term a lot because you can exorcise a demon from a person without the power of God. However, deliverance is a term that is exclusive to the Christian faith. Deliverance not only includes the casting out of demons, but it also addresses emotional wounds, fragmented souls, soul ties, and one's difficulty in extending forgiveness.

Why aren't more churches teaching deliverance?

I have no concrete answer as to why so many Christian churches avoid deliverance. I can only share my thoughts regarding this topic. It is my belief that people are afraid of anything dark and cynical, and the mere fact that most people cannot see demons makes it even more terrifying. The church is comprised of these very people, and they would rather teach around the edges of deliverance or completely avoid it as a result. The church has a big mouth but at the core, she truly does not understand her authority. I grew up in one of the most conservative churches in the world, who prides herself on keeping The Ten Commandments and being God's remnant people. Even in her prideful courts, deliverance is avoided like the plague. Speaking of pride, prideful Christians do not want to admit that they are demonized. They would much rather struggle privately than risk being exposed publicly.

In addition, some churches just do not know where to start when it comes to deliverance. So, they do absolutely nothing instead of seeking help. There are churches where the pastors work overtime to discredit the work of deliverance. They teach that it is not necessary because giving attention to darkness will ultimately bring unnecessary trouble in your life. They even go so far as to say that pursuing such acts gives the enemy too much credit. They do not realize that they have been deceived and are guilty of deceiving others. Nevertheless, I am in constant praise of God that more and more churches are beginning to wake up to the power of deliverance. Thankfully, they have come to the understanding that deliverance will cause a church to blossom and explode in power.

Did Jesus deliver?

Absolutely! Jesus spent his years of ministry preaching, healing the sick, and casting out demons. As a matter of fact, Jesus stated in Mark 16:17, "…and these signs will accompany those who believe: In my name they will drive out demons…" (NIV). It is settled! Jesus expects us to cast out devils in his name.

What should I expect?

No two deliverances are the same. However, I would like to prepare you for what I call demon intimidation. Do not be surprised if they show up in your dreams or whisper in your ears that you should avoid deliverance all together. Some might even be bold enough to tell you that deliverance should be avoided because your deliverance minister is a witch or some agent of darkness. I have heard it all! Do not be frightened by the horrifying nightmares you will have after you decide to pursue deliverance. The dreams are designed to scare you and cause you to abort the process. Your demons know they have but a short time before they will be commanded to go, so they will stop at nothing to deter you from being free. Expect to feel anxious and nervous. It is normal. You are now venturing into new territory, so try your best to relax. The end result will be FREEDOM from demonic bondage.

What if my family is against deliverance?

Do not expect everyone to support your decision. Actually, it is best to keep your decision private. A lot of people shy away from deliverance because they are deterred by family members, friends, and church members who are skeptical of deliverance. I always tell people not to seek counsel about deliverance from people who, more than likely, need deliverance themselves. You already know something is off in your life, and the only cosigner you need is the Holy Spirit.

Will the demons hurt me?

No, the Holy Spirit orchestrates the deliverance process and he protects you. I keep referring to Luke 10:19 which says, *"Behold, I give unto you power to tread on serpents and scorpions, and over all the power of the enemy: and nothing shall by any means hurt you."* If you notice, there is a protection clause included, and it states, *"...and nothing shall by any means hurt you."* You may feel some discomfort as the demons are manifesting and leaving but nothing that will cause you harm. Rest assured, your experienced deliverance minister will know how to handle those demons that become testy.

What if they tell my secrets?

There are some demons that will rattle off secrets. Demons will use your fear of embarrassment to keep you from opening up during deliverance or to get you to abort the deliverance process. However, I would not worry about it. More than likely, they have been able to torment you with those very secrets. Exposing them frees you and breaks their hold on your mind and life. A demon can use a secret as a legal right because you cannot confess or forgive what you will not acknowledge. In a private deliverance session, confidentiality should be guaranteed so that your exposed secret will not be allowed to travel outside the session. Overall, your mindset should be on breaking free no matter the cost.

How will I manifest?

It is very difficult to predict how you will manifest. No two people manifest the same way. Some demons manifest and become rather chatty while others manifest and refrain from saying a single word. However, their presence is obvious. There are some that will just get up and leave without making a spectacle. Demons may manifest and cause headaches, trembling, facial contortions, eye twitching, or a choking sensation. Another manner in which they may manifest is by causing pain in one's arm, chest, neck, stomach, and/or back. When exiting your body, they may leave through burping, vomiting, yelling, sneezing, yawning, coughing, tears, a runny nose, or through a desire to urinate or defecate.

Will I be aware?

It is hard to tell because everyone is different. Some people are aware of the deliverance process but are unable to control it, while others report that they were not aware of anything until the demon actually left and the deliverance minister addressed them.

What should I look for in a deliverance minister?

You should look for a deliverance minister who is experienced and well versed in spiritual warfare. This individual should be a devout servant of the Most High God, confessing that Jesus is Lord and is the only way to our Father, God. It should not be a requirement for you to purchase anointing oil or any trinkets from them that relate to deliverance. In addition, a safe environment for deliverance should be offered to you. Finally, they should require that you fill out some sort of assessment or at least, take the time to learn as much about you as possible before administering deliverance.

It is my requirement that a one-hundred question assessment is completed prior to walking a person through deliverance. This assessment tool helps me identify the areas of demonic oppression operating in an individual's life. It also assists me in successfully educating the person about the tactics and strategies the enemy has been using to kill, steal, and destroy in their life. The assessment also assists me in providing the individual with vital strategies necessary for maintaining their deliverance once they have been set free.

In my opinion, no one should attempt to walk you through deliverance without knowing as much as possible about you and your family. Furthermore, one must know how to appropriately assess the information supplied on the assessment. If you think about it, the majority of services you receive in life require an assessment of some form. For example, when you go to the doctor you must share information about you and your family. An assessment is also completed when you get your car serviced. Your mechanic would never approach repairs on a 1966 Ford in the same manner as he would a 2016 Ford.

Assessments are administered so that your deliverance process is individualized and tailored to your specific situation.

Should I pay for deliverance?

Some deliverance ministers charge a fee while others speak strongly against it. Please understand that every deliverance minister is different. You can never pay for deliverance, but you can compensate a person for their time and knowledge base. Experiencing deliverance in the comfort of your home is priceless. In my mind, you pay more to travel, hotel expenses, food, and offering if you choose to attend a conference.

Personally, I charge for one-on-one sessions and my classes because I do more than administer deliverance. Each session is at least three hours long. I am a clinically licensed, (masters-level) social worker, and I incorporate my expertise into the sessions that I administer as well. Secondly, charging a fee helps me weed out those who are not serious about breaking free. There are currently more than 40,000 people on my page, and not everyone who reaches out is serious. In the past, I lost hours that I can never more retrieve by investing in individuals who truly were not serious. My fee helps to deter those types of individuals. My conference calls, prayer lines, mass deliverance sessions, memes, and inspirational posts are free. At the conclusion of the matter, you must pray and do what the Holy Spirit leads you to do.

How should I prepare for deliverance?

I would suggest that you dedicate at least 24 hours to fasting and praying. Prepare mentally by visualizing yourself free. Quote Luke 10:19 and John 10:10 every chance you get. Get into a posture of thanksgiving. Tell God thank you again and again for setting you free. Make sure that you make provision to be alone or at least educate everyone who will be around of what to expect.

How do I keep out the demons that leave?

Demons are kept out by your living a life of Holiness. Regular Bible study, fiery prayers using the weapons of warfare, and abstaining from sin is crucial. Lead a repentant life. Pray in the spirit. Faithful church attendance or surrounding yourself with other believers is also very important. Build and maintain your relationship with Christ. Rely on and depend on the fellowship of the Holy Spirit as your guide. Monitor your dreams and cancel anything that Jesus does not agree with. Lastly, watch the company you keep.

Will everything leave the first time?

It is the goal of every deliverance minister to target the strongman and to get all of the lower-ranking demons to follow him out. Most of the time we are successful, and other times it takes several rounds of deliverance to get everything out. This is very common as it depends on the person and what they are dealing with in their personal lives. Demons can hide behind fragmented souls and soul ties. However, every case is different. Keep in mind that deliverance is progressive. I usually encourage people who come to me for private deliverance to take my class instead because it is very comprehensive. Not only do I teach you about spiritual warfare and address your emotional strongholds but also I walk you through several rounds of deliverance.

How do I know I am delivered?

You will immediately feel lightness in your body. Besides that, another huge indicator will be the freedom you experience in your mind, will, and emotions. I often say that deliverance will free your mind so that you can use your mind. However, in my opinion, the most powerful indicator of them all is when you transfer into the realm of a more abundant life. The greatest sign requires lots of fiery prayers but the end result will be the release and return of the things that were stolen from you.

How long does deliverance take?

Once again, every case is different. I always ask those with whom I am privileged to work with to allot at least four hours for deliverance.

What can block me from getting delivered?

There are several reasons that a person's deliverance can be blocked or hindered. Let us examine the reasons in the list below:

1. Church members, pastors, friends, and family members speaking doubt or insisting that you do not need deliverance.
2. Failure to repent sins.
3. Harboring a fear of retaliation from demons.
4. Unaddressed legal rights such as unforgiveness, resentment, and hatred.
5. Blockages because of an undiscovered fragmented soul.
6. A need to be in control of the deliverance process and refusal to relax long enough for the demons to manifest.
7. Using deliverance as an avenue to fulfill a selfish desire (i.e., seeking deliverance to win the heart of a lover). Please know that God will not be used.

What are the methods that can be used to deliver me?

You can be delivered face to face, over the telephone, or via Skype. All means are effective. The Holy Spirit is not bound by time or distance.

Can I deliver myself?

Most deliverance ministers agree that you cannot deliver yourself from the strongman. You need help getting him out. Once he is gone, you can utilize deliverance prayers to eradicate other lingering demons.

Who seeks deliverance?

People from all walks of life, economic statuses, and cultures seek deliverance. Seekers are not bound to one gender or age group. Anyone who desires to be set free will be set free when the Holy Spirit comes for them.

Have I ever experienced deliverance?

You already know!

Soul Work:

After reading this book are you convinced that demons are real? Why or why not?

If yes, what are the chances that you would walk through deliverance with someone?

Prayer:

Father God, I receive the authority that you left me in Luke 10:19.

Prayer Point:

I decree and declare that deliverance is my portion.

Put a Ring on Your Journey

Chapter 17

It is very easy for people who do not understand spiritual warfare or anything about demons to automatically assume that anyone who dares to study the matter is perhaps, drifting to the dark side. Trust me, I know. People were very suspicious of me when I began my journey. Thankfully, I was in a place where I could truly afford not to care. I lived by myself and was solely responsible for the ins and outs of my life. I could boldly shut down without giving an account to anyone. However, you may not be in such a place. You may be married or sharing a dwelling place with people who count on you, or you on them. You may be catching grief from the person to whom you are committed, a family member, your best friend, a church member, or even your pastor. Relax and be patient with them. You must understand that what you know is an internal knowing. They did not receive the revelation you received, so it is pointless to argue your point. Do not share things in hopes of receiving validation or affirmation. At this juncture, God is calling you and not them. This journey is about you, so allow it to transform you and your fruit will shut the mouths of the lions. My love, no one has to agree with you or understand your plight.

Let me add, you may become obsessed with the information you learn. More than likely you will find yourself studying every chance you get. You are okay, and it is part of the process. Your spirit is drinking. You will begin to see the world through a magnified spiritual warfare lens. You may begin to feel overwhelmed at times, and when you do, take a step back and rest. The hunger will resume and as time goes on, your elevated urge to label everything evil will subside but your pursuit of righteousness will not. You are literally carrying your cross while in hot pursuit of God.

Be prepared as you may lose some support and relationships that you value deeply. Just remember that nothing will leave your life that was meant to stay. You may be asked to leave your current church as you awaken to the hunger for meat rather than milk. All I can say is this, keep your ear to the heart of God and be prepared to obey. Stay in His face. You will have moments when the weight of your elevation may seem overwhelming. You may even feel that you are losing your mind. Rejoice, for your breakthrough is nigh! Spiritual warfare will remove every person and thing that does not belong in your life and replace it with those people and things that do. Bank on it!

You have come to the point in your journey where you are ready to renounce and break every evil covenant hanging over your life. The prayers in the following appendix are dangerously powerful and will destroy most legal rights and weaken the spirits at work in your life. These prayers cannot only be used to weaken and cast out demons but also be used to maintain your deliverance. Please be advised that depending on the depth of your oppression, you will need assistance calling stronger spirits out of your body. Seek out a knowledgeable and experienced deliverance minister. Last but not least, I want to reinforce the fact that deliverance is a process that YOU WILL WIN IF YOU FAINT NOT. Once again, I can hear you wondering if this process is the real deal, Ha! You already know!

Appendix A
Prayers to Break Covenants

1. Poverty

Father, I recognize that the spirit of poverty has attached itself to me and it must be eradicated. Poverty is sorely affecting my quality of life and I am not having it. I am its prisoner and that's not ok with me. Whatever I or my ancestors did to make this spirit so comfortable in my life, I reject it now with the blood of the lamb. I saturate with the hot boiling blood of Jesus, every oath, covenant, pact, sexual orgy, blood sacrifice, act of betrayal, pathological dishonesty, perpetual misuse of money, time and talents that opened the door for the spirit of poverty to enter my bloodline and my life. God, I ask that you will extend forgiveness to my ancestors who ushered iniquity onto the bloodline that seduced this wicked spirit. I too extend forgiveness for I know that it's necessary. I send the fire of God to uproot and set ablaze every word uttered from my mouth, every transaction made into the enemy's life from my hands, every blown opportunity to be a financial blessing, and every seed planted in poor ground that has allowed the spirit of poverty to grow and continue devouring my finances, time and talents. Poverty, I bind you and I command you to die by fire right now, in the name of Jesus! Poverty, your legal rights to operate in my life are no more and I command you to pack your bags and leave NOW. Poverty, you are the thief that I have identified and accuse before the Father. I command you to obey the policy of Proverbs 6:31 and return into my hands sevenfold everything that you have ever stolen, blocked, and delayed from me and my ancestors! Release it right now in the name of Jesus and die! Amen

2. Cycles of Defeat

In the name of Jesus, I command every demonic cycle occurring in my life to be broken! I renounce and denounce you and refuse to dance to your evil cycles any longer! I take authority over the sun, moon and stars and command the programmed cycles of defeat to backfire and be eradicated from my life by the fire of God! I will tolerate you no more! I take authority over my body, soul and spirit and I command you to wake up and fight back. Refuse the demonic cycles that dare to devour your time, derail your destiny and make your existence on earth of no significance.

Jesus, according to your divine authority, I ask that you stand in the middle of every demonic cycle with my name on it and command, "Peace, Be Still!" No longer will I find myself in the same position year after year, month after month or day after day because God has released the spirit of the breaker to smash, dismantle and annihilate every cycle of defeat that has been operating in my life in the mighty name of Jesus! Amen

3. Limitations

In the name of Jesus, I REFUSE to be limited by demonic entities who have been assigned to frustrate my life. Limitations contradict the freedom that Jesus paid for humanity to have. By the divine authority of Jesus Christ, I demand my release and the expansion of my borders! Limitations, I command you to be limited and destroyed by the fire of God! In the name of Jesus, I demand that every enemy to my destiny be bound and eternally removed from my life right now. I blood slap every Pharaoh that desires to hold me captive and lock me in a spiritual box; loose me NOW in the name of Jesus! I release the spirit of the breaker to go forth and once again, blood slap you. I command the sledge hammer of the Lord to smash, dismantle, and annihilate your boundaries. Limitations, I command you to know me nor my address any more! Father God, I pray according to 1 Chronicles 4:10 that you will bless me, enlarge my borders, and continually protect me from all evil in Jesus' name. Amen

4. Delay

I speak to the spirit of delay and I command you to break your hold over every area of my life in the name of Jesus! Your works in my life are disrespectful to the established will of God for my life. I disagree with your assignment and I repel your presence with the shield of faith! I command you to flee and to be forever delayed from operating and lurking in my life! By the divine authority of Jesus Christ, I command a tsunami of the blood of Jesus to flow into every area of my life that you are affecting. In the name of Jesus, drown upon contact! Amen

5. Demonic Hauntings

Every demonic power haunting my dwelling place, be haunted by the power of the Holy Ghost! I command the exposure of your hiding place. I command you to leave my home NOW in the name of Jesus! You are not welcome here! I refuse to share my physical or spiritual dwelling place with anything that is unclean. Every curse that has hijacked my home, break in the name of Jesus! Holy Spirit, you and you alone are welcome here. Sweep my whole house with your spiritual broom. Leave no room, crevice, or corner unturned! Leave no remnants of unclean spirits in my home in the name of Jesus! Every power that does not want me to have peaceful rest in my home, I command you to be buried now in the name of Jesus. From this point moving forward, I will have sweet sleep, rest and safety in my home in Jesus' mighty name. Amen

6. Dreams

God, I had a dream that I absolutely do not agree with. Everything about the dream contradicts your plan for my life and my answer is absolutely NO! Evil dreams, you are rebuked! I saturate you in the blood of Jesus and command that you be consumed by Holy Ghost fire. I break every demonic covenant and contract that I unlawfully entered into while I slumbered. I also command my spirit to regurgitate all food and drink consumed. The works of dark powers attacking my dream world will not manifest in my life. I reject all evil covenants that usher blockage, poverty, sickness and disease, limitations and delay into the various areas of my life. I blood slap you and refuse to be reinstated into old demonic covenants that I have already broken. I order every dream snatcher to return my dreams NOW! Return them to me safely and without delay. Holy Spirit, help me recall all meaningful dreams and deal with each appropriately. May your blood forever serve as an eraser and protector of my dreams. Amen

7. Accidents

In the name of Jesus, I break and nullify every covenant, oath, and pact that is hanging over my life, designed to cause accidents of all kinds in my life. Daily I soak myself and all of my possessions (name them) in the blood of Jesus. I flash my shield of fire designed by God to repel all accidents that intend to harm me, my family, my home, and my possessions in the name of Jesus! Assignments behind all accidents in my life, I renounce your assignment, and command you to catch fire and die NOW in the name of Jesus! I challenge and destroy your death assignment with the fire of God. Powers frustrating and fighting against my life, die in my place. Accident causing spirits shall trouble me no more because the blood of Jesus is now operating as my Passover. Amen

8. **Addictions**

Let's get this straight; nothing has the right to hold me captive but the power of the Holy Spirit and even He does so by my will. Therefore, every addiction troubling my life and robbing me of my peace, divorce your legal right and flee in the name of Jesus. I curse you from the root up along with your evil manifestations in my life. I renounce and denounce you and command you to break your evil assignment immediately! Whoever or whatever gave you the authority to trouble my life, you will honor their instructions and covenants no more! My body is the temple of the Holy Ghost and your controlling and demanding ways are unwelcomed. I break your hold from over my life NOW by the blood of Jesus! I will not bend or bow to your pull any longer. Forget my name, abandon your post, and leave my body NOW in the name of Jesus! Amen

9. **Emotional Turmoil**

I confess that I have the mind of Christ. Therefore, all spirits troubling my life, I command you to die by fire! I rebel against your assignment to manipulate my mind, will, and emotions. In the name of Jesus, I reject the spirits of depression, anxiety, anger, suicide, confusion, sorrow, rage, isolation, and extreme loneliness by severing all ties with you foul spirits! I confess that the Holy Spirit is my Comforter and that God will never put more on me than I can bear. I command you evil assignment of emotional turmoil to carry your own load and die! All witchcraft induced oppression, I command you to break your hold and abandon your post. I reverse your effects and command you to go oppress your sender NOW in the name of Jesus! I command your lies to be uprooted from my mind, will, and emotions. I command the spirit of Truth to be released in the places you once occupied. Where you had internal torment, I have the peace of God. In the name of Jesus, flee from my body NOW! Amen

10. Health Issues

Evil loads of sickness and disease, abandon your post immediately in the name of Jesus! You are in direct violation of what the word of God declares over my body, and have made a mistake by troubling my body and my peace! I confess and renounce every door that I opened and command it to be closed eternally! I renounce and denounce every wind of sickness and disease sent to me by friendly foes, household wickedness and my carelessness. I command the assignment to be broken off me and reversed to the evil sender! I command you to render unto them what was meant for me. I declare war in the heavens against you and your power in the mighty name of Jesus! I eradicate and trump every legal right with the blood of Jesus. Spirit of infirmity, I cast down your witchcraft sponsored infirmity in the name of Jesus! I shall not die but live and declare the works of the Lord in the mighty name of Jesus! Amen

11. Chronic Rejection

In the name of Jesus, I renounce and curse the spirit of rejection that is hanging over my life, and I command you to wither up and die in Jesus' name! I boldly snatch off my forehead the letter "R" that specifically attracts people and circumstances into my life with the assignment to reject me. I command the spirit of rejection to be rejected in the name of Jesus! By fire, I expose all residue and eradicate them from the root in the name of Jesus! Holy Ghost fire, scan me and ensure that no residue of rejection is left in my body. Rejection you are rejected and ejected in the name of Jesus. I receive the full acceptance and love of God in your place! Amen

    a. Self-Rejection - I forgive myself for believing the lies of the enemy that taunt and whisper that I am not enough in any area of my life. I forgive myself for the many ignorant and bold mistakes that I made in life. I find rest in knowing that nothing that I have done or ever will do will take God by surprise. I am the apple of my Father's eye; I am above and not beneath; I am the head and not the tail; I am loved and accepted; I am highly favored; I am fearfully and wonderfully made. There is nothing that will ever separate me from my Father's love. Amen

b. Rejection of Others - I repent and receive the forgiveness of God for the people that I have rejected in my lifetime. I soak every occurrence in the blood of Jesus. The memories of my actions will no longer be able to haunt my mind and cause condemnation to taunt me. Even if the subjects of my rejection refuse to forgive me, I will not be held bound by their unforgiveness. I release myself from what the blood of Jesus has already covered. Amen

c. Mother - Mother, I choose this day to forgive you for rejecting me. I forgive you for not being there to nurture and instruct me as a mother should have. I forgive you for giving me to relatives to be raised. I forgive you for choosing men and your lifestyle over me. I forgive you for the word curses that you spoke over my life. I forgive you for not teaching me the true meaning of womanhood and servitude. I forgive you for not taking better care of your body and succumbing to sickness and disease. I forgive you for sexually violating me. I forgive you for not being there to shield me from being sexually violated by family members and friends. I forgive you for not speaking up and protecting me. I understand that your brokenness caused you not to be there for me. I understand that as a product of your bloodline, you were the best mom that you could be. I understand that you could not communicate the way I needed you to because no-one taught you how. I understand that you gave me all the love that you had to offer. I understand that things happened to you that were outside of your control and you took them out on me. Even so, I forgive you and break all word curses that you spoke over my life. I break myself free from every generational curse passed down by your blood line with the blood of Jesus. Amen

d. Father - Father, I forgive you for rejecting me and not loving me the way that I needed you to. I forgive you for not being there to raise me and protect me as a father should have; I forgive you for choosing another family over me. I forgive you for only coming around only when it suited you. I forgive you for not teaching me the way that I should be treated by men. I forgive you for not being my hero. I forgive you for sexually violating me. I forgive you for not being there to shield me from being sexually violated by family members and friends. I extend my forgiveness to you even if you do not offer me yours. I understand that you were not able to be the father that I needed you to be because of your own bloodline and open door issues. I no longer harbor any resentment against you. I now choose to look towards the future and not dwell on the past. In Jesus' name. Amen

e. Others - In the name of Jesus, I forgive every family member and friend who rejected me (call their names out loud), and I release you from the prison of my heart. I choose not to harbor any negative feelings towards you. I replace every thought and feeling towards those who rejected me with the love of God. I forgive former and current educators and employers who rejected me (call their names out loud). I release you from the prison of my heart. I choose not to carry you anymore. Amen

12. Family Destruction

In the name of Jesus, I command every evil spirit that is fighting my family's unity to flee in the name of Jesus! I send the blood of Jesus back four hundred generations in order to eradicate the legal rights that brought and established generational plagues of confusion within my family. I send the blood of Jesus to raise a higher altar in the place of the demonic ones erected. I command the fire of God to burn into ashes the memory of every iniquity embedded in the bloodline's DNA and replace it with the DNA of our heavenly Father. Familiar and monitoring spirits, track us no more in the name of Jesus! I send the fire of God to blind you and to send you into a state of permanent confusion thusly rendering you useless! In the name of Jesus, I bind the spirits of confusion and offense and release the spirits of peace and unity. I command the bloodline blessings to chase down and overtake me and every family member who not only loves but obeys the Father. In the name of Jesus, the negative bloodline traits and behaviors that we were once known for are now cancelled. Surely mercy and goodness shall follow our bloodline from now until the close of our earthly chapter. Amen.

13. Romantic Relational Issues

Every spirit behind my romantic relational struggles determined to keep me single, trouble me no more in the name of Jesus! I issue you a divorce decree and render you single. I reject you and your demonic covenant. I want absolutely nothing to do with you. I command your covenant rings to be destroyed by the fire of God. I am no longer your candidate for marriage so beat it. I break the yoke of every spirit pressing me to settle for less than God's best for my life. I will marry up. Stubborn powers, I bind you and command you to carry your own loads of just enough, almost, rejection and confusion. Return back to your sender NOW in the name of Jesus. Render unto them what was intended for me! I command your demonic veil to be ripped from off of my face and to be consumed into ashes by the all-consuming fire of God! I command every blood sacrifice made on behalf of my marital destiny to be consumed by the fire of God. Every coven agenda blocking my marital destiny, I command your death by fire in the name of Jesus. Amen

14. Sexual Humiliation

I command every witchcraft power assigned against my life to carry your evil load of sexual humiliation and die! I forbid you in the name of Jesus from touching my body ever again! If you touch my body, you will touch the fire of God. I uproot your DNA and scent from my body in the name of Jesus! I prohibit every witchcraft spirit from using my body against God's will! I command every witchcraft spirit assigned to disrespect my body to die NOW in the mighty name of Jesus! I decree and declare that my body is the temple of the Most High God. I confess that my body is filled with the Holy Spirit, and it shall be used to advance the Kingdom of God. I renounce and eradicate all feelings of shame, unworthiness, condemnation, and guilt from my soul in Jesus' name! Father, cover my trauma with your blood and heal me from the root up in Jesus' name. Amen

15. Fertility Issues

Father, this day I present my maternal and paternal bloodlines before you. I repent on behalf of my ancestors who brought iniquity onto the bloodline, specifically causing fertility issues. I cleanse my bloodline with the blood of Jesus. I send Holy Ghost fire to burn up every contract, covenant, oath, and pact that my ancestors established with the enemy! Enemy, I refuse your works and report. I anoint my womb with the oil and fire of God! I command anything planted in my womb by witchcraft powers to burn into ashes! Be uprooted and surrender to the fire of God. Every witchcraft plan and attack against my womb, be scattered by fire right now in the name of Jesus! I break your covenant of destruction, and I command you to surrender to the fire! Holy Spirit rise up in your power and disgrace my enemies. I confess that my womb is blessed and not cursed. I claim Hannah's anointing over my life and womb in the mighty name of Jesus. I declare and decree that motherhood is my portion in the name of Jesus. Amen

16. Spiritual Blockage

I eradicate and dismantle every spirit operating against my spiritual destiny whether under the earth, in the water, in the air, and roaming the land. I abort your assignment sent to trouble and harass my spiritual destiny for the sake of causing me to question and dishonor God. May the angels of God stone to death every spirit whose assignment it is to lead me into idolatry and self-worship. I suffocate with the hand of God every spirit that is blocking my ability to hear God's voice! I curse the accusers of God for their attempt to pressure me to blame God for the negativity in my life and the world. I seal the lips of the enemy by sewing them together using the needle and thread of the Most High God! I refuse the spirit of the antichrist and a strange voice I shall not follow. I command my release from every demonic prison! I refuse to remain a blind prisoner and command my soul to demand its release. I refuse all demonic foods and sexual advances in my dreams! I regurgitate all demonic foods eaten knowingly and unknowingly in the name of Jesus! All evil deposits in my body designed to weaken me spiritually, may your weapons be reversed and backfire! I command the arrows of the enemy to return unto him and pierce him in the heart! I command you to die by heart failure in the name of Jesus! I confess that I belong to the Most High God and anything contrary to His will for my life, must be consumed by Holy Ghost fire! I decree and declare that the Lord is my strength and He will continue to strengthen me spiritually, physically, and mentally. Amen

17. Limbo

In the name of Jesus, I defy and curse the assignment of limbo on my life. Jesus Christ died for me to move forward in life and anything that attempts to hold me in one place, void of progression, is spiritually illegal. I speak to every rope tied around my waist causing me to tread in place, burn by fire. I speak to every demon who specializes in attracting people and situations into my life that feed your assignment, choke and die in the name of Jesus. I speak with fire to all witchcraft powers responsible for burying, freezing and/or placing a lid on my progression and advancement, break your hold and live your own evil pronouncements! I demand all dark assignments of limbo to catch fire and lose your ability to operate in my life for ever! Limbo rope and assignment, burn by fire. Progression and advancing by fire is my portion. In the name of Jesus, I release myself from your hold of non-progression and non-advancement. I free myself by the blood of the lamb from your demonic treadmill. I'm progressing and advancing at supernatural speed. Amen

18. Use Me

I break the "USE ME" curse from over my life with the Power of God. Whatever was done— be it through me, my ancestors, or an evil foe— to cause individuals to use me and neglect to bless and honor me, I command it to be dismantled by the blood of Jesus. My support, gifts, acts of service, affection, love, affirmation, Godly-counsel, intercession, money, time, and goodness are valuable in the sight of God, and so shall they be in the sight of man. No longer will people render my goodness with evil nor take my presence for granted. People will pour into my bosom and look for ways to promote and honor me appropriately. My star will not be buried nor transferred to another because it will only respond to directives from the Most-High God concerning me. Use me curse, make yourself useful and die in the name of Jesus. I declare that I am growing in wisdom, stature, and favor with God and man daily in Jesus' name! Amen

19. Sabotage

Curse of sabotage, you are destructive to my character and your works are absolutely unacceptable! I will NOT tolerate your works ANY MORE! I send the anaconda of the Most High God to wrap itself around you and slowly squeeze the life out of you! While bound by the anaconda, the angels of God are retrieving all that you stole from me because of a tainted reputation that you created! The Holy Spirit has personally reversed your damage and erased all stains associated with my name. The Holy Spirit has uprooted your lies and replaced them with truth in every area of my life. Spirit of sabotage, you must repay me sevenfold for what you caused. I release warrior angels to enforce my sevenfold return. Spirit of sabotage, I call for your early judgment, and command the anaconda of God to swallow you whole! Sabotage, the twins Grace and Mercy dethrone you from where you comfortably reigned; they now follow me everywhere that I go. In Jesus' name, Amen!

Appendix B
Breaking Self - Imposed or Imposed Upon Curses

1. Someone Gave Your Bloodline Over

Holy Spirit, walk up and down my mother's bloodline, my father's bloodline, and locate every relative that summoned and fed demonic strongholds on the bloodline. Lord God, please forgive them for their wicked acts, and I too extend forgiveness for suffering the consequences of their iniquity.

Lord God, I humbly ask that you soak their dirty deeds, every oath, covenant, and pact with your blood. Wherever there is a blood sacrifice, whether human or animal, cover it with your blood. Let your blood violently locate and trump every legal right that the enemy is using to accuse my bloodline. I send the fire of God to consume into ashes every area where I sent the blood of Jesus. Let the blood of Jesus serve as gasoline be set ablaze by the fire of God. As a descendant of the bloodline, I stand and take my rightful place as a radical generational curse breaker, ready to take my life of abundance by force. I renounce and denounce the enemy's rights to me and my family. I eradicate it by fire, by fire, by fire! I eradicate it by fire, by fire, by fire! Break your hold in the precious name of Jesus! I take it by force, by force, by force! I take it by force, by force, by force! Amen

2. Friendly Foe

Father God, in the name of Jesus, please expose my friendly foes. Empower me with the discipline and boldness to release them when expose them. I stand in authority decreeing and declaring that their weapons formed against me shall not prosper. Please wipe their memory database clean of all information regarding my life. I send the fire of God into their meeting places to burn to ashes everything therein regarding my life. I command the angels of God to snatch back every word curse, negative thought, and poisonous action being committed against me. I send the blood of Jesus to saturate them completely, and the fire of God to consume them in the name of Jesus. Amen

3. Offense

Father, please forgive me for the things that I have said and done, both knowingly and unknowingly, that has offended others. Father, it is never my intent to harm anyone. Please cover me with your blood and cause the arrows of offense that are being shot at me to fall down at your feet and be consumed by Holy Ghost fire. I command all witchcraft to die by fire! I refuse to walk in offense and release those whom have offended me. Spirit of offense, what are you waiting for? Uproot yourself and commit suicide in the name of Jesus! Amen

4. Crab Curse

I command the curse of the crab to be eradicated from my life in the name of Jesus. I send the sword of God to cut off all of your legs and arms rendering you helpless. Your assignment in my life no longer works. I command you to turn on your sender! I slip from out of your grip with ease in the name of Jesus. From this moment moving forward, I rise to the top unhindered. Favor of God, I am ready. Locate me now and do a great work in Jesus' name. Amen

5. Sexual Violation

Witchcraft powers assigned against my life, I command you to carry your load of sexual aggression and die. I forbid you to disrespect my body through others ever again. I uproot your hate and rage from my life with the love of Christ. Violate my body again and you will violate God and receive his wrath. Holy Ghost cleanse every scent and DNA deposit from my body in the name of Jesus. Touch my body, and you touch fire. Witchcraft embargo against my body, die in the name of Jesus! Amen

6. Word Curses

By the divine authority of Jesus Christ, I release the spirit of the breaker to dismantle, smash, and annihilate the power of the curses spoken over my life by (insert name) who said (insert curse). I renounce the power of the curses and command the blood of Jesus to saturate and permeate them. I command my warring angels to locate in the atmosphere every word curse that has been spoken over my life, and to violently snatch them down in the name of Jesus. I call forth every single person associated with speaking such devastating words over my life, including myself. I disagree with your poisonous words and render them powerless. I boldly renounce every negative word ever spoken over my life. And as I view these words, I pronounce them as lies and not the truth. Satan is the father of lies, and I do not embrace his words as truth because they operate against the divine will and order of God for my life. I spray each word with the blood of Jesus and set them ablaze with Holy Ghost fire! Those words will no longer prevent, hinder, or delay my soul wounds from healing or soul ties from unraveling. They will no longer hide behind unforgiveness, resentment, pride and hate. I render these words that were sent to weigh me down and to destroy me as powerless. They no longer have any authority to affect, control or oppress me. I uproot you from my mind and command you to die by fire! I speak the truths of God concerning my life. I refuse to be held captive any longer by the opinions and offenses of others. I forgive and release (insert name) from the prison of my heart in Jesus' name. I release my ministering angels to remove each arrow from my heart and dagger from my back. Every wound is filled with the flesh of God and healed by Jesus' stripes. Father, I ask that you release your ministering angels to begin writing scriptures of love on my heart. May the beautiful and perfect words of Jesus take root and explode in my life forevermore. Amen

7. Guilty By Covenant or Association

How can two walk together except they agree? God please forgive me for being unequally yoked with individuals who do not live for you. I renounce these relationships and vow to break them off immediately. By the divine authority of God, I disassociate myself with these individuals. I break every attack of the enemy as a result of these evil associations with the hammer of the Lord. I blood block the enemy's ability to find me in the spirit realm. I am protected by the blood of Jesus and no weapon formed against me will prosper. I call on the fire of God to purge me of all evil influences, deposits, and remnants from these associations. I renounce any verbal agreements, pacts, and oaths that I have made to uphold these associations until death in the natural realm. I command the angel of the Lord to snatch them out of the atmosphere, and to throw them down onto the ground; breaking them into a million pieces. Holy Spirit, act as a vacuum cleaner, suck them up, and discard of them in the fiery furnace where they will be burned into ashes. Wind of the Most High God scatter them into a million directions in the mighty name of Jesus, never more to be reconciled. Amen

8. Open Doors

I slam shut every open door in my life that has left me open and vulnerable to the attacks and infiltration of the enemy. Father, I ask your forgiveness for walking in ignorance, disobedience and rebellion against you. It is my desire to live in humble obedience to you and according to your perfect will. Through the divine authority of Jesus, I am slamming all open doors shut; never to be reopened. I send Holy Ghost fire and the blood of Jesus to act as sealants. My mind is made up that you are my Lord and Savior. I refuse to turn back. Nothing from the enemy's camp is my portion. I renounce lust and sexual perversion in all forms, witchcraft in all forms, lying, stealing, addictions, unforgiveness, pride, and any other behaviors contrary to your nature. Powers of darkness holding me hostage to my past, SCATTER by fire! I am a new creature. The Lord has granted me the power and ability to forget those things behind me, and to press forward in Him. I have the victory and will finish strong in the name of Jesus. Amen

9. Secret Societies

Father, I ask that you bring to my remembrance any secret society ties, occult practices, or ungodly commitments that my family knowingly and/or unknowingly made that are affecting my life. Lord, please forgive my ancestors for their ignorance and willful disobedience. I repent for ignorantly joining (insert name). I renounce and denounce all covenants that I entered into through the oaths and pacts that I verbally agreed to. Under the power of God, I snatch back my covenant establishing words and signature and render them null and void. I surrender my mind, body and soul strictly to the God of heaven and earth. I break all associations with (insert name) and vow to destroy all items that tie me them. Through the divine authority of Jesus, I break the curses from over my life and I command the blood of Jesus to saturate and permeate every area of my life. Amen

10. Demonic Games and Activities

I renounce and denounce all demonic games and activities that I have engaged in knowingly or unknowingly. I saturate the memory in the blood of Jesus. I erase all traces of my involvement with the enemy's record. I send forth God's all-consuming fire to destroy all evil contracts, oaths, covenants, and pacts with my name on them. I repent for my involvement with Ouija boards, horoscopes, palm readings, fortune tellers, hypnotism, and any other practices of the occult. Holy Spirit, intercede on my behalf and break the yoke of bondage from over my life. I will no longer conform to the ways of the world, but be transformed by the renewing of my mind in the mighty name of Jesus. Amen

11. Abortions

Lord God, I repent for aborting my unborn child/children. I acknowledge that life is precious and ordained by you. I committed murder by agreeing to endure such a barbaric act. Lord God, please forgive me and everyone directly involved with the act. Lord, please forgive every person who had knowledge of what I was going to do and did not try to stop me. Lord God, please wipe my record clean and let not the blood that I spilled be used as a blood sacrifice by ancestral or witchcraft spirits. Trump the spilled blood with your blood. Please disconnect me from the condemning consequences of my actions. I forgive myself and I vow to never dishonor my body with such a demonic practice ever again. Lord, I receive your forgiveness and move forward casting guilt and shame behind me forevermore. Amen

12. Fornication and Sexual Perversion

God, I repent and ask your forgiveness for giving my body sexually to persons that are not my spouse. I acknowledge that fornication is a sin and that my body is the temple of the Holy Spirit. I repent for allowing ignorance, pride, rebellion, rejection, the influence of my environment, society, and brokenness to cause me to give my body away carelessly. In the name of Jesus, I seize and take back every covenant that I made with the spirits of sexual perversion and lust as a result of my behavior. This day, I offer my body to you as a living sacrifice and send the blood of Jesus to wipe my sexual history clean. Spirits, I have no business with you. Leave my body NOW! I repent on behalf of my ancestors that ushered such spirits into the bloodline. I renounce all bloodline spirits of sexual perversion and lust. Ancestral spirits, forget my name and leave my body NOW! I send the fire of God to sweep my body clean and to reclaim it for the glory of God. I refuse to be a slave to lust or sexual perversion. Holy Spirit, I cannot consistently win this battle with my flesh without you. Now that my body has been called back unto you, I receive your instructions, guidance and restoration. Amen

a. Fornication - Lord God, I present my body to you as a living sacrifice which is my reasonable service. Father I ask forgiveness for mistreating and defiling my body by participating in premarital sex. I acknowledge that sex is an act preserved solely between a married man and woman. My body belongs to you until such a time. I apologize to the people that I fornicated with and I apologize to myself. I call my bodily fluids back to my body, and I rid my body of their bodily fluids by the fire of God. Lord God it is my desire from this moment on to live a life of celibacy in deed and in thought. I command every demon of fornication, lust and perversion that attached itself to my life as a result of my transgressions to leave my body now. I no longer belong to you. In the name of Jesus, I resist you and evict you from my life permanently. Amen

b. Pornography - Father I must confess that I have an addiction that has me by the throat. I was introduced to pornography and now the pornography bug has spread in my life like wildfire. It has consumed me and no amount of positive confessions or prayer that I've prayed so far seem to help. Father, it calls me and demands a sin offering at the most inopportune moments. Father, I now know that pornography is a form of sexual perversion and I hate it. This perversion is not only in me but on my bloodline too. Father, I renounce everything that my ancestors did in order to invite and feed the spirit of perversion. I refuse to allow what's sitting on my bloodline calling my name with the intent of destroying my life to remain any longer! Father, I repent for cooperating with my bloodline demons by opening the door and partnering with them. I renounce and denounce every covenant that I entered into with them. Through the blood of Jesus, I cover my ancestor's evil acts and mine with the blood of Jesus. I send Holy Ghost fire to consume those acts. The legal right is no more and they must go! I refuse to allow the spirit of addiction that came in with perversion to stay in my life. Father, I need you to touch my life this day and evict these spirits and their residue from out of my life completely. Dry them up! Drive them out with your power! I know that I must do my part by building my spirit man, monitoring what I entertain and acquire an accountability partner in order to support me. God, I receive my deliverance by faith. Amen

c. Incest - Father, I ask for forgiveness for the acts of incest that I engaged in willingly and unwillingly. I acknowledge that incest is offensive to you and is a form of sexual perversion. I extend forgiveness to family members who violated me sexually and I apologize to family members whom I violated. Lord, I ask you to cleanse my body and blood from the memory of incest. I receive your cleansing power and forgiveness. Amen

13. False Religions

In the name of Jesus, I renounce and denounce all false doctrine and religions that I have ever entertained and/or practiced in my life. I command the poisonous root to be uprooted and destroyed in the name of Jesus. All confusion that you brought into my life must be eradicated by Holy Ghost fire. I accept Christianity in its purest form. I root out any deception with the bloodhounds of God. I bind and cast out every spirit of the anti-Christ, death, hell and the grave in Jesus' name. Amen

14. Trauma

Father God, I lift up my life to you. I command your spirit to operate as a flash light that will search for any brokenness caused by traumatic experiences. I command the fruits of abuse and rejection to be exposed now in Jesus' mighty name. I send the angels of the Most High God to close the doors and gateways of trauma so that the enemy can no longer torment or afflict me. I seal the door shut forever with the blood of Jesus. I send the fire of God to consume into ashes all of the legal rights that anger, depression, fear, shame, sickness, panic, grief, anxiety, and hopelessness have to operate in my life. Be scattered by the wind of the Most High God. By the divine authority of Jesus Christ, I command every root of trauma operating in my life to loose your hold on me NOW. You have no more power. I send my warring angels forth to uproot you and cast you into the red sea of death. I break your hold from over my mind, will, and emotions. I renounce and cast down every thought and lofty imagination that is not of God. I decree and declare that I have the mind of Christ. Your accusations and ridicule will no longer haunt, torment, or oppress me. I shift the blame back to you, and I command you to die by fire in the name of Jesus. I forgive those whom you have operated through to violate me mentally, physically, and/or emotionally. I set them, and myself free from bondage as I will no longer cosign with rebellion and unforgiveness. I decree and declare that I have been healed from brokenness, my spirit restored, my heart cleansed, and set free from captivity. I am healed by the stripes of Jesus who died on the cross for me. Amen

15. Drugs and Alcohol

My body is the temple of the Holy Ghost. I repent for abusing my body with illegal drugs, excessive prescription pill usage, and the over consumption of alcohol. I also repent for turning to drugs and alcohol for comfort. As written in 1 Peter 5:8, "I am to be alert and be of a sober mind." Father, I command your fire to consume every unclean desire that I have for drugs and alcohol. I break all generational curses of addiction donated to me from my mother's bloodline and my father's bloodline. I decree and declare that I am free from the judgments of others, their condemnation, and rejection of me. I release my offenders of any and all unforgiveness that I have held onto from past hurts and offenses. I forgive and release (insert name) from the prison of my heart. I command the angels of the Most High God to write scriptures of love on the tablets of my heart. I am free to walk in love with all men. Father, I thank you for breaking the strong grip of rebellion from over my life. I blood block all strategies, tactics, and tricks used by the spirit of rebellion to seduce me back into a life riddled with unforgiveness, depression, anger, rejection, pride, hate, and arrogance. I send Holy Ghost fire to cleanse my blood and burn out all impurities left behind as a result of my alcohol and/or drug consumption. Father, make me whole again. I command all spirits of addiction to leave me now in the name of Jesus. I refuse your enslavement and break every covenant that my ancestors and I have made with you. Your assignment over my life is over in the mighty name of Jesus. My broken heart has been healed and I am no longer oppressed, but free to walk in the liberty proclaimed by Jesus Christ according to Luke 4:19. Amen

16. The Devil's Entertainment

There is nothing good that flows from Satan. He is the father of all lies and it is his job to pollute all that is righteous. Therefore, I renounce and denounce the enemy's entertainment. Lord, give me the strength and the will power to resist the temptations of the enemy concerning my choices of entertainment. Holy Spirit stand guard at the gates of my eyes and ears day and night. I give him permission to cut down any fiery darts that are thrown my way. I send fire to root out the seeds of the anti-Christ that have already been planted in my mind and soul. Satan, I will sow into your kingdom no more. I decree and declare that

I desire to listen to and view Godly entertainment only. No longer will I be bound by the seductive ways of the enemy through music, television programs, concerts or books in the mighty name of Jesus. I slam this door shut and command it to be sealed with the blood of Jesus. I command all wicked powers roaming about and going uncontested in my life to die by fire in the name of Jesus. Holy Spirit intercede on my behalf and break the yoke of bondage. I decree and declare that I am free from the love of demonic entertainment by the divine authority of Jesus Christ. Amen

17. Gossip

Father, in the name of Jesus, I repent for the evil words that I have allowed to escape from my mouth and to flow through my ear gates. I uproot all evil communication and break all agreements with the enemy. I crucify my ears and mouth. Lord, I place them on your altar to be corrected. I command my ears to entertain good tidings and truth only. I decree and declare that my words will damage the kingdom of darkness instead of building it. In the name of Jesus, may every witchcraft entangled tongue rising against me be forever silenced. May the fire of God locate and extinguish every lie, gossip, rumor, slanderous word, and plot propelled against me. According to Isaiah 54:17, I condemn every tongue that has risen against me. I blood block any negative words and lies from entering my ear gates in the name of Jesus. From this day forth, I command my mouth to speak blessings and not curses. I decree and declare that my words will be used only to edify and not to destroy in the name of Jesus. Amen

Appendix C
Prayers of Renunciation

1. Soul Tie (Chapter 9)

Holy Spirit, I ask that you search my soul and reveal those soul ties that have me entangled in their demonic knots. Every demonic tie holding my soul captive, I rebel against you now in the name of Jesus. Your tie is not freedom and I demand my release by the divine authority of Jesus Christ. I send forth the spirit of the breaker to shatter, smash, and annihilate your hold from over my life. I repent for my participation, whether by choice or force, in any ungodly sexual relationships in the past and present. No longer will I be bound to ex-lovers (state their name(s)) and their lovers. I sever all ties with these individuals with the scissors of the Most High God. I blood block all thoughts and feelings associated with these toxic relationships with the purifying blood of Jesus. I command the sword of God to break me free from the North, East, West and South. Jesus died so that I could walk in authority and freedom. I demand the release of my mind, my will, and my emotions in the mighty name of Jesus. Amen

2. Spiritual Sex Trafficking (Chapter 9)

My body belongs to the Most High God and not a spirit spouse. It is illegal for a spirit to marry a human. This day, I issue you a divorce decree, and command all wedding paraphernalia to be consumed by Holy Ghost fire! I command all of your evil deposits made in my body to be purged by the blood and consumed by Holy Ghost fire! I use the blow torch of God to burn your rings from off of my fingers. I am not your spouse. I resist and deny you! Any claims that you have to my life are weak and hold no merit. You are not wanted or loved. Spiritually speaking, I am the bride of Christ and He's possessive and jealous concerning me. Spirit spouse, I renounce and denounce your works concerning my life. Be blood slapped and die. Amen

3. Spirit Children (Chapter 9)

In the name of Jesus, I abandon and reject any and all spirit children that I have with the spirit spouse! Spirit children, I command you to be malnourished and killed by the sword of God! Die now! Die now! Die now! I command the earth to open up and swallow you whole! Be swallowed up! Be swallowed up! Be swallowed up! Amen

4. Familiar Spirits (Chapter 2)

I command every familiar spirit visiting me in my dreams in the form of dead relatives and sending masquerading spirits with the assignment of reinforcing bloodline curses to be exposed by Holy Ghost fire! I disconnect myself from your evil family covenants. In the name of Jesus, I command scales of deception to be ripped from my eyes and ears! I divorce myself from my mother and father's bloodlines. I partner with the bloodline of Jesus Christ. Familiar spirits check my lineage and the only name that you will see is that of Christ. I reject you and accuse you before the Father! Be exposed now and die! Be exposed and die! Be exposed and die in the mighty name of Jesus! Amen

5. Soul Wounds (Chapter 10)

Father, I lift up my soul to you. It has taken quite a beating over the years. It's filled with bruises and holes that I need you to address. Father, I've experienced so many traumas throughout my life. I know that I must move past my pain. To be honest, I thought I had, but my soul has not. I still experience a lot pain and continue to walk in unforgiveness in those areas where I thought I had forgiven, healed, and moved on. My soul is in need of your healing touch. Come now

Lord God to where I am and pour out your healing virtue upon my wounds. I don't want them anymore. I can't afford them and I cannot continue to carry them. The burden is just too much to bear. They must go! Father, you instructed the weary and heavy laden to come unto you and you will give them rest. Well, Father, here I am; surrendering all to you. I am wounded and in need of your healing touch. I command the puss releasing infection to ooze out. I release your blood to flow in and to saturate and permeate every inch of my soul. I command the maggots feeding on my infected and dying flesh to choke on your blood. Father, cleanse each wound from the base up. Fill every hole with your flesh. Father, I release your hammer to smash and break the hold of every traumatic memory that's operating in my life to keep me in bondage. Spirit of Pharaoh, I demand my release now! I command my ashes to be transformed into beauty. I bind, renounce, and cast out of my body every demonic entity that is hiding behind my pain in the name of Jesus. You cannot continue to use my body as your safe haven. Get out of my body NOW! Your legal right is no longer valid. Die by fire! Lord God, thank you for revealing and healing every soul wound housed in my body in Jesus' name. Amen

6. Witchcraft (Chapter 12)

In the name of Jesus, I break myself free from every witchcraft initiation. I do not and will not agree with my name or body being used for the kingdom of darkness. Whoever gave my name over, gave it over illegally and I'm contesting it. I serve notice today that I belong to the Most High God and as a result, may your evil works backfire in the name of Jesus. I curse your works at the root and command them to wither up and die in the name of Jesus. Everything in the witch's cauldron pot, be consumed by Holy Ghost fire. Every blood sacrifice made on my behalf, be erased and replaced by the blood of Jesus. I disconnect myself permanently from witchcraft and all of its works. Wherever my name is being called and it's not of God, may the Holy

Spirit answer for me. In the name of Jesus, witchcraft backfire and lose my name!

Appendix D
Prayer Points Against Demonic Dreams

1. **Sex**
   a. In the name of Jesus, every demon raping me in my sleep, be exposed and swallowed up by the earth.
   b. Every demon violating my body be violated and destroyed by the sword of God.
   c. All deposits made into my body, be consumed by Holy Ghost fire.
2. **Getting married**
   a. Every demonic power claiming me as their bride, die by fire!
   b. Spirit husband/wife, be made a widower/widow by the fire of God.
   c. Spirit spouse, wearing a ring on my behalf, catch fire and die.
3. **Snakes**
   a. Every serpent spirit tracking my life, be coiled into Holy Ghost knots and die.
   b. Serpentine spirit disturbing my peace, drink the blood of Jesus and die.
   c. Python spirit sent to delay me, be delayed by the power of God. Uncoil yourself and die.
4. **Coffin**
   a. Spirit of death plotting against my life, may your plans backfire in the name of Jesus.
   b. Spirit of death, where is your sting?! Die by Holy Ghost fire.
   c. Instead of dying, I shall live and declare the works of the Lord.
5. **Sitting for an exam repeatedly**
   a. Repeated struggles tracking my life, lose your way and die by fire.
   b. Programmed struggles attached to my life, detach yourself and die.

c. Every repeated struggle popping up in my life, be plucked out and die by fire in the name of Jesus.

6. **Reoccurring dreams**
   a. Every reoccurring dream, be satisfied by the wisdom of God.
   b. Every reoccurring dream, be stopped by the strategy of God.
   c. Every reoccurring dream, doing me harm, be eradicated by the fire of God.

7. **Stolen, missing, or spotted wedding dress**
   a. Every power attacking my marital destiny, be struck down by the lightning of God.
   b. Water spirits claiming my marital destiny, drown in the blood of Jesus.
   c. Every attack against my wedding garments, die by fie.

8. **Blocked doors**
   a. Witchcraft powers sitting at the edge of my breakthrough, scatter by fire.
   b. Blocked doors, be unblocked by the fire of God.
   c. Power of God, knock down every blocked door refusing to open up to me.

9. **Kissing or Being Kissed**
   a. Kiss of betrayal, be betrayed by the power of God.
   b. Every spirit of betrayal plotting against me, be exposed and arrested in the name of Jesus.
   c. Every evil covenant sealed with my kiss, be destroyed by the fire of God.

10. **Reoccurring dreams of past events and/or places**
    a. In the name of Jesus, I live in the now and not the past.
    b. Every spirit holding me in the past, break your hold in the name of Jesus and die.
    c. Troubles from my father and mother's house, forget my name. Lose my scent and die in the name of Jesus.

11. **Dead relatives**
    a. Familiar spirits posing as my dead loved ones, be exposed and roasted by the fire of God.

b. Ancestral spirits enforcing evil curses and soul ties in my life, die by the blood!
  c. Familiar spirits, posing as dead relatives, be bound and tossed into the pit.

12. **Strange creatures fighting you**
    a. Strange creatures fighting me in the night, I punch you with the fist of God.
    b. Strange creatures disturbing my rest, be exposed and consumed by the hot lava of God.
    c. Strange creatures determined to harass me, be harassed by the warrior angels of God.

13. **You see yourself rising and suddenly falling**
    a. I will rise and not fall because the hand of God upholds me.
    b. Every demonic power tracking to demote me, be struck down by the power of God
    c. Evil power assigned to watch me rise and to make me fall, be aborted by the power of God.

14. **Stolen shoes**
    a. Wherever my shoes are being hidden, I command them to be located and returned to me now in the name of Jesus.
    b. Evil powers, get out of my way. I will carry the gospel unhindered in the name of Jesus.
    c. Spirit of poverty claiming my life, I command your assignment to backfire in the name of Jesus.

15. **Stuck in traffic**
    a. Every witchcraft power blocking my progress, die by fire.
    b. Holy Ghost power, push me past my stuck place in the name of Jesus.
    c. Dark powers blocking my traffic, get out of my way and let me pass in the name of Jesus.

16. **Seeing yourself naked**
    a. Demonic shame assigned to attack my life, backfire in the name of Jesus.
    b. Where I am naked, the Lord God clothes me.

c. Shame from the house of my enemies, backfire in the name of Jesus.
17. **Slow-moving creatures:**
   a. Demonic slow progress, break your hold from over my life in the name of Jesus.
   b. Holy Ghost wind dry up the assignment of slow movement and propel me forward.
   c. Slow moving progress, be put to shame by the acceleration of the Lord Jesus Christ.
18. **Chained or imprisoned**
   a. Chains of imprisonment operating against my life, die in the name of Jesus.
   b. Jesus died to set the captives free, I demand my release now in the name of Jesus.
   c. Let every prison door operating against my life by opened now by Holy Ghost fire.
19. **Repetitive dreams of an old place of employment**
   a. Old place of employment, your season is over in my life, release me in the name of Jesus.
   b. Demonic entities blocking my promotion, die by fire.
   c. Soul wounds from my old place of employment, be healed by the blood of the lamb.
20. **Always arriving late**
   a. Every hindering spirit delaying my arrival, die by fire.
   b. Spirit of delay, drink the blood of Jesus and croak.
   c. In the name of Jesus, door of opportunity open speedily
21. **Rats and roaches**
   a. Spirit of poverty, be bankrupt and die by fire.
   b. Unclean spirits, carry your filthy load and die by fire.
   c. In the name of Jesus, I refuse to share my wealth with anything unclean, die by fire.
22. **Stolen seat**
   a. Every stolen opportunity of rest, return to me now in the name of Jesus.

    b. Every demonic power fighting against my settled place, be uprooted and embarrassed.
    c. The Lord God placed a chair before me in the presence of my enemies, I will rest.
23. **Crying**
    a. Every demonic plot designed to draw water from my eyes, backfire in the name of Jesus.
    b. Every tear caused by demonic powers, turn into a sea and drown my foes.
    c. Spirit of sorrow, lose my scent and carry your own evil load. Backfire in the name of Jesus.
24. **Sexual orgies, porn, homosexual acts, or exposure of sex organs**
    a. Every evil sexual assignment sent to pollute my life, be demolished by the blood of Jesus.
    b. Spirit of perversion, be perverted by your own powers and die in the name of Jesus.
    c. My body is the temple of the Holy Spirit and the winds of perversion shall not prevail.
25. **Losing blood**
    a. Every blood thirsty spirit drinking my blood, drink the blood of Jesus and die.
    b. Demonic entries after my life, die by fire.
    c. Blood thirsty powers of darkness, drink your own blood and eat your own flesh, in the name of Jesus.
26. **Seeing old lover(s)**
    a. Lover from my past, our time is up, unravel your tie and flee in the name of Jesus.
    b. Unnatural soul tie, shrivel up and break in the name of Jesus.
    c. Lovers from my past, I eradicate our tie and command your influence in my life to die by fire.
27. **Driven by an unknown person to an unknown destination**
    a. Unknown person, show your face and be destroyed by the power of God.

b. Unknown person, abort your assignment and leave my vehicle now in the name of Jesus.
   c. I am the driver of my own destiny; unknown driver, give me my keys and die by Holy Ghost Fire.

28. Roaming aimlessly
   a. Every evil compass controlling my life, be destroyed by the hammer of God.
   b. The steps of a good man are ordered by the lord, God order my steps.
   c. Evil wind of witchcraft blowing me to and fro, be silenced by the wind of God.
   d. My legs will carry me to my place of destiny unhindered.

29. Someone cutting or shaving off your hair
   a. Oil of divine protection and covering come upon me now.
   b. In the name of Jesus, the glory of God will never escape my life.
   c. Demonic devices used to shave my hair and rob me of my glory, jam and explode in the name of Jesus.

30. Someone straightening your hair
   a. In the name of Jesus, the uniqueness of my glory will never fade.
   b. In the name of Jesus, I refuse the enemy's plot to make me common.
   c. Demonic conspiracy to give me a common destiny, and common glory, I curse you at the root. Wither up and die.

31. Being shot or chased
   a. Bullets from the enemy's camp, backfire in the name of Jesus.
   b. Demonic powers on my heels, I trip you with the leg of God.
   c. In the name of Jesus, bullets from the kingdom of darkness touch my shield of faith and fall to the ground.

32. Ants, rats, roaches, tattered clothing, losing property, finding coins, spending money, or losing your purse or wallet
   a. You disgusting assignment of poverty against my life, die by fire.

    b.   Light of God, locate the thief of darkness and demand the return of my stolen goods.
    c.   I am a part of the beloved kingdom of God where poverty is not my portion.

33. Losing or damaging your phone
    a.   I command the arrest of every demonic entity operating against my heavenly signal.
    b.   All demonic powers sent to attack my prayer life, be destroyed by Holy Ghost fire.
    c.   Jesus is on the main line and every assignment sent to block our call must be eradicated by the blood.

34. Losing teeth
    a.   I have the wisdom of God and it shall not be disturbed.
    b.   Every agent of darkness aiming to sift my wisdom, fall down and die in the name of Jesus
    c.   Every demonic assignment sent fight against my wisdom, backfire in the name of Jesus.

35. Drunkenness/Alcoholism
    a.   Spirit of addiction, swallow your addiction and die in the name of Jesus.
    b.   Every spirit counting on my drunkenness in order to enter my body, become drunk by the blood of Jesus and die.
    c.   I am alert and sober minded to do the will of God.

36. Hit on the head
    a.   Witchcraft power requesting my sanity, go insane in the name of Jesus.
    b.   In the name of Jesus, neither insanity nor confusion will EVER be my portion.
    c.   Mind control witchcraft, I have the mind of Christ and refuse your control in the name of Jesus.

37. Spider webs
    a.   Every demonic spider web waiting to trap my life, burn to ashes by Holy Ghost fire.

    b. Every demonic web of false doctrine be exposed and corrected in the name of Jesus.
    c. Spider web traps, backfire and entrap your sender in the name of Jesus.

38. Spiders
    a. Every demonic spider spewing rejection into my life, be rejected in the name of Jesus.
    b. Demonic spider of witchcraft lose your legs and die in the name of Jesus.
    c. Demonic spider releasing venom in my life, be injected by your own venom and die.

39. Often swimming or bathing in large bodies of water
    a. Every marine demon claiming my life, be consumed by Holy Spirit fire.
    b. Water surrounding the marine demons in my life, drain and be replaced with the blood of Jesus.
    c. In the name of Jesus, marine demons boil in the blood of Jesus.

40. Fighting with family or friends
    a. Every demon behind my family confusion, let your confusion backfire and tear down your kingdom.
    b. Every demon behind friendship confusion, let your confusion backfire and tear down your kingdom.
    c. Demonic powers fighting my family unity, choke and die in the name of Jesus.

41. Ants
    a. Every demon determined to work me without profit, die in the name of Jesus.
    b. In the name Jesus, working without profit is not my portion.
    c. Every assignment to work me without fruit, I command you to go back to your sender in the name of Jesus.

42. Dogs
    a. Every spirit of perversion, die by fire.
    b. Every witchcraft spirit, go kill yourself in the name of Jesus

c. Witchcraft spirit, I refuse your wind of fear and intimidation in the name of Jesus.

43. Cats
  a. Every spirit of betrayal lurking in my life, lose my address and die by Holy Ghost fire.
  b. Every familiar spirit, lose your mind and die by fire.
  c. Every spirit of darkness creeping in my life, be exposed and decapitated by the sword of God.

44. Shopping but not locating your size
  a. Whatever I seek, I shall find in the name of Jesus.
  b. My portion of blessings must be exposed to me now in the name of Jesus.
  c. The table of plenty shall be presented unto me wherever I go in the name of Jesus.

45. Animals chasing you
  a. Animals chasing me in my dreams, I slay you with the sword of God.
  b. Animals behind disturbing my rest, be exposed and embarrassed by the power of God.
  c. Animals creatures determined to harass me, be harassed by your own powers.

46. Constantly running
  a. I command the treadmill curse to cease and desist in my life in the name of Jesus.
  b. I curse the demonic program in my life to block my rest and keep me running.
  c. I run, walk, jog, and rest only when instructed by God.

47. Missing a flight
  a. In the name of Jesus, I refuse to miss any destiny moments.
  b. Every demonic arrow shot at me to delay me, back fire in the name of Jesus.
  c. Every demonic power fighting against my destiny, I anoint you to kill yourself.

48. Missing keys
   a. In the name of God, I reclaim my missing keys from the kingdom of darkness.
   b. I tuck my keys of authority close. Enemy you will not steal from me.
   c. I recover my authority and utilize them to overthrow the powers of darkness.

49. Police
   a. Every ancestral spirit sent to arrest my destiny, die by fire.
   b. Every demonic policeman sent to hijack my anointing, be arrested by the power of God.
   c. I resist the arrest of demonic spiritual policeman, and command them to desist in the name of Jesus.

50. Seeing items disappear from your life
   a. In the name of Jesus, I demand the return of everything that has been stolen from me.
   b. I chain down, with the power of God, everything that the enemy is after in my life.
   c. My portion that you have stolen from me, be released by fire.

51. Eating
   a. In the name of Jesus, I regurgitate everything that I have ever eaten in my dreams
   b. Judgment of darkness against my life feeding me in my dreams, die by fire.
   c. Blood of Jesus purge my body of all demonic brew.

52. Blocked by a large body of water
   a. Water from the marine kingdom dry up now in the name of Jesus.
   b. Marine kingdom blockage, be blocked by your own water in the name of Jesus.
   c. Marine Kingdom daring to trouble my life, be consumed by my God's holy anger.

53. People laughing at and mocking you
   a. To all of my mockers, check my fruit and mock me no more

b. Oh God arise and wow my mockers with your presence in my life.
   c. Oh God, where my mockers and accusers are, they are no more.

54. Broken items or damage to property
   a. Demons of destruction touching my life, I touch you with the hand of God. Be paralyzed and break.
   b. Daily I cover my possessions with the blood of Jesus.
   c. Any demon that touches my stuff touches fire!

55. Robbery
   a. I demand the return of everything that has been stolen from me.
   b. I chain down, with the power of God, all that the enemy is after in my life.
   c. My portion that you have stolen from me is released by fire.

56. Frogs
   a. Spirit of the frog, pack your contaminates and hop away in the name of Jesus.
   b. Every foul and unclean spirit polluting my life, die by fire.
   c. Frog spirit, I cut off your legs and embarrass your assignment in the name of Jesus.

57. Alarm clock going off
   a. Every alarm clock sounding in my life, cut off now in the name of Jesus.
   b. Time consumers and wasters, be consumed by fire.
   c. The Lord has shown me favor and added years unto me.

58. Music played that seduces you
   a. I refuse the devil's rhythm and will dance no more.
   b. Demonic music sent to seduce me in my dreams, lose your rhythm and tone. Die by fire
   c. Spirit of darkness trapping me with your music, may your music turn into hymns in the name of Jesus.

59. **Talking to strange people and traveling to strange places**
    a. I only respond to the voice and directives of God in my dreams.
    b. I command my soul and spirit to travel only to the third heaven.
    c. I command my soul and spirit to rebel against the directives of the powers of darkness.

60. **Accidents**
    a. I eradicate all accidents sent to frustrate and destroy me in the name of Jesus.
    b. In the name of Jesus, I refuse to operate in fear of having an accident.
    c. All accidents waiting for me, backfire in the mighty name of Jesus.

61. **Miscarriage**
    a. The fruit of my womb is protected by the blood of Jesus, and a miscarriage shall not be my portion.
    b. Nothing that God places in my life shall be aborted but carried to full term.
    c. Spirits of Lilith and Molech lurking to steal my seed, die by fire.

62. **Being hit in your pregnant belly**
    a. The fruit of my womb is protected and a miscarriage shall not be my portion.
    b. Nothing that God places in my womb shall be aborted but carried to full term.
    c. Hand of the enemy sent to strike my seed, wither up and die in the name of Jesus.

63. **Giving birth to or suckling an unknown child that you believe to be yours**
    a. Demonic spiritual child sucking up my virtue, be malnourished and die.
    b. Demonic baby sucking up my milk of plenty, may my milk be laced with the blood of Jesus. DIE!

c. Demonic entity calling me mommy, I reject and orphan you in the name of Jesus. Die by fire.

Minister Faithe would like to personally invite you to connect with her on The Power Pusher's Facebook, Twitter, and Instagram accounts.

Please visit The Power Pusher's website at: www.thepowerpusher.org for more information regarding the ministry and services.

www.ingramcontent.com/pod-product-compliance
Lightning Source LLC
Chambersburg PA
CBHW070637100426
42744CB00006B/717